PROJECT MANAGEMENT

Lessons from the Field

CARL PRITCHARD, PMP®

iUniverse, Inc.
New York   Bloomington

*PMP® is a registered service mark of the Project Management Institute, Inc.
of Newtown Square, Pennsylvania*

iUniverse books may be ordered through booksellers or by contacting:

iUniverse
1663 Liberty Drive
Bloomington, IN 47403
www.iuniverse.com
1-800-Authors (1-800-288-4677)

ISBN: 978-1-4401-5649-6 (sc)
ISBN: 978-1-4401-5650-2 (ebook)
ISBN: 978-1-4401-5651-9 (dj)

Printed in the United States of America

iUniverse rev. date: 9/11/2009

Contents

Abbreviations and Acronyms

AACE	Association for the Advancement of Cost Engineering
AFTRA/SAG	American Federation of Television and Radio Artists/Screen Actors Guild
ANSI	American National Standards Institute
APM	Association for Project Management
ASAPM	American Society for the Advancement of Project Management
BCWP	Budgeted Cost of Work Performed
BCWS	Budgeted Cost of Work Scheduled
BJCP	Beer Judge Certification Program
BS	bachelor of science
CCCM	Certified Commercial Contracts Manager
CDP	Certified Data Processor
Certified MBTI	Certified Myers–Briggs Type Indicator Professional
CFCM	Certified Federal Contracts Manager
CFP	Certified Financial Planner
CIO	chief information officer
CPA	Certified Public Accountant
CPCM	Certified Professional Contracts Manager
CPE	Certified Professional Estimator
CPI	Cost Performance Index
CSDP	Certified Software Development Professional

CV	curriculum vitae
ESTCP	Environmental Security Technology Certification Program
EVMS	earned value management system
EVP	Earned Value Professional
FAQ	frequently asked questions
FDR	Franklin D. Roosevelt
FFP	firm fixed price
FTP	file transfer protocol
GAAP	Generally Accepted Accounting Practices
IEEE	Institute of Electrical and Electronics Engineers
IPMA	International Project Management Association
ISO	standard of the International Organization for Standardization
IT	information technology
LPIC	Linux Professional Institute Certification
MBA	master of business administration
MBO	management by objectives
MCSE	Microsoft Certified Systems Engineer
MoT	moment of truth
NAPM	National Association of Purchasing Management
NASA	National Aeronautics and Space Administration
NDA	nondisclosure agreement
PERT	program evaluation and review technique

PM	project management
PMBOK® Guide	*A Guide to the Project Management Body of Knowledge*
PMI	Project Management Institute
PMO	project management office
PMP	Project Management Professional
POGO	Project on Government Oversight
QMS	quality management system
RBS	risk breakdown structure
RFP	request for proposals
SEI	Software Engineering Institute
SOX	Sarbanes–Oxley
SPI	Schedule Performance Index
STS	Space Transportation System (space shuttle)
TPM	technical performance measurement
TQM	Total Quality Management
UPS	United Parcel Service
WBS	work breakdown structure

INTRODUCTION

Project management (PM) is a profession that is seemingly without boundaries. Project managers take it upon themselves to apply project management to everything from weddings to multibillion-dollar efforts to crack the frontiers of science. And it's all still labeled "project management."

The intent of this book is not to create boundaries for the profession, but instead to draw upon the insights of more than twenty years of application in the field from the simplest projects to the most leviathan. Originally, these articles were created for www.projectconnections.com. The intent was to tackle the issues of the day in such a way that there are applicable nuggets from every article and insights from personal, student, and professional experience. There is no single focus for this book save that of project management.

The articles are arranged so you can read through them from a process perspective. If you prefer to read them from a *Project Management Book of Knowledge (PMBOK® Guide)* (Project Management Institute 2008) perspective, refer to the table at the end of the introduction. Or, by using the index, you may simply ferret out articles that are germane to your pressing situation or subject area.

The emphasis here (as with project management) is on practical application. Most project management texts tend to focus on the narrow mechanics of the profession, without shedding light on the repercussions of those mechanics in the day-to-day workplace. Still other texts pontificate from an academic perspective. They suggest lofty tools and applications that have academic merit but limited utility in the field. This collection strives to bridge the gap of practicality and applicability from a real-world perspective.

What makes great applicability? When you can see

yourself in the situation. When you can understand and empathize with the environment described. When you have the capacity to envision how and when you might adopt (or adapt) the practices described to make yourself more effective and to make your day run more smoothly. Those are the best business practices you can find. To the degree possible, that's what I've tried to capture through the years in my articles.

Each article is accompanied by the original month and year of publication to provide perspective on the timing of the discussions and the events going on in the world around us. Several articles tie back to the historic events of 9/11, both when they were fresh in our minds and in the years hence. Some of the lighter articles are tied to the time of year or to holidays. Several Christmas and Halloween articles are provided as a break from the headier discussions on the profession. Some of the older articles have been refreshed with more current (2009) information to make them germane to the current project environment.

My intent for the collection is to provide perspective on the work that we do and how we do it and the practical frustrations and triumphs associated with our work. There are few things on Earth that provide greater solace than to know someone else has shared our experiences and can provide alternative views on how to cope with those experiences. There is also a sense of affirmation when we know that those around us can lay claim to the same joys we experience at a well-laid plan, a successful delivery, or a team member's success. Across the span of more than a decade of articles, I've attempted to capture those experiences.

The lack of boundaries in project management sometimes creates the illusion that we are alone in the work we do. Because the frontier is so vast, it is occasionally daunting to try to find the other pioneers. We should strive to look for the commonality of our experiences, the lessons learned, and the empathy that can evolve through a shared story line.

About the Author

Carl Pritchard, PMP, PMI-RMP, EVP is a thought leader in project management and one of the lead chapter authors for the Guide to the Project Management Body of Knowledge, 4th edition. He has written books on the work breakdown structure, risk management, project scheduling, and project communications, and coproduced the 9-CD Audio collection *The Portable PMP Prep* with J. LeRoy Ward. He is the U.S. correspondent for the British project management magazine, *Project Manager Today*, and serves on the board of directors for ProjectConnections.com.

Carl lectures around the world to audiences on topics ranging from effective consulting to risk management ethics. He is a highly sought-after trainer and dinner speaker and regularly presents entertaining webinars and on-line programs in connection with the Project Management Institute.

He and his wife, Nancy, are the cofounders of Pritchard Management Associates of Frederick, Maryland. Together, they have spent more than a decade serving project management clients large and small, providing project support through entertaining education and on-the-ground consulting. They can be reached through the corporate Web site at www.carlpritchard.com.

Acknowledgments/
Dedication

Working as an independent consultant for more than a decade means that I have relied on a host of people and organizations through the years, each helping me build a practice that I like to believe reflects both best practice and a genuine interest in the best possible outcomes for each person I work with. For this book, however, I must acknowledge one organization above the rest—ProjectConnections.com. The articles included here have been crafted and edited through the years and have appeared on the ProjectConnections.com Web site. They have encouraged me to professional excellence and have provided insight and guidance. To Cinda Voegtli and Deanna Burghart, I offer my sincere thanks and appreciation.

I also must acknowledge my local editor, Sue Deavours. She continues to illustrate that there are editors and then there are editors of project management material. She knows the profession and its history, and that is an invaluable resource in this type of effort.

Above all, however, I acknowledge my wife and sons. My wife is a source of stories, support, insight, and guidance. With her interminable patience and coaching, she provides perspective on the human side of the equation that I would often otherwise miss. She is a partner in every true sense of the word, and I appreciate her for it. For my sons, James and Adam, I acknowledge their contributions both through the years of stories and through their willingness to tolerate a father who, on occasion, has been known to be a bit of a blowhard. They keep their Dad in check.

This book is dedicated to Nancy, my wife and partner.

Contents by Knowledge Area

Process: Initiating

Under Construction: Template Development for Project Managers

Developing Structures That Can Make This Project (and the Next and the Next) More Effective

(November 2000)

Project organizations regularly wrestle with the notion of whether to build or buy templates to suit their organization. In some cases, they come to locations like www .projectconnections.com to borrow templates and modify them to meet more specific needs. But for many project managers, there are no templates. And rather than build them, they go through what's sometimes referred to as the Band-Aid approach and build project information structures from scratch for each project individually. It gets frustrating. It wastes time.

The counterargument is that templates allow us to become lazy. They encourage project managers to simply reapply the same old approaches, whether they were deemed effective or not. Some boilerplate practices are done time and again not because they're particularly effective, but because they're built into a template. There are strategies to develop templates well and to build them in a short time. The key is to know what the templates are supposed to accomplish.

Setting Template Goals

Frequently, when organizations decide to build project management infrastructure, they turn to consultants. They should take a lesson from those consultants and invest the time in assessing the needs of the users and determining what the users really hope to accomplish. The questions are simple: What problem do we hope to solve? What information do we want to capture? What repetitive practice do we hope to preclude? If there are no clear, simple, and direct answers to those questions, there is no hope of building a template that will serve the need. In an amazing twist, many organizations will adopt forms and templates without considering the needs they hope to address. And then, they are dissatisfied with the outcomes.

The sequence is crucial. The needs are identified, and *then* the templates, forms, or protocols are developed. As we identify the needs, we need to ensure that the information requested is crystal clear. Identifying project status as an informational need is not sufficient. Which elements of project status are important? And how do we want to see them? Project status can be expressed in terms of dates, percent complete, percent spent, work remaining, customer satisfaction to date, or a host of other criteria. We need to define those criteria that are most important to our organization, which then allows us to refine the sources of those data and the realism of the potential template application.

Breadth or Depth

How much information is appropriate for a given template? Some organizations strive to build templates that embed huge volumes of data. Others strive for simplicity. For organizations just starting out in the realm of building templates or internal protocols, simpler generally is better. Ideally, the data should be available from a common source. The template should address a single issue or data need. And the template should be information that is otherwise not available in a synthesized fashion. The template must bring information together in new ways and must draw out new insights. If the goal is simply a recapitulation of information available elsewhere that can readily be drawn out, there's no need to build a new template to access it.

Some templates bring out information previously unavailable. If so, data formatting becomes all the more important. The data must be cataloged in a way that makes the information accessible not only to the user of the template but also to others who may need the information.

Next Steps

After you've identified the data needs and an effective format, the keys become accessibility and access. Be it paper or virtual, as they say with the real estate market, the issue is location, location, location. If we can find a common repository for the forms and the completed templates, we make great strides in our ability to share information. One organization that has followed through on this principle is ProjectConnections (the original host site for these articles). It builds and shares templates common across industries and across a variety of practices. Given that the major requirement is a file transfer protocol (FTP) Web site with password protection, you have the opportunity to build similar libraries of project templates and information for you and your organization. By providing a resource that works well and is readily available, we can build on a shared resource and take advantage of the insights and history of others.

* * *

The Great Salesman: How to Sell What We Do Without Selling Out

Defining the Project Management Sales Pitch

(March 2001)

The argument is often made that to sell what we do for a living, we have to sell a small part of our souls. People should recognize project management for what it is. They should embrace it as we have. They should honor, revere, and respect it as we do. And then ... *they don't!* It's appalling. They don't have the good sense to acknowledge that we are working as the guardians and protectors of time, cost, and requirements. Salesmanship is not necessarily an innate trait for many project managers. And some project managers don't perceive themselves as great salespeople. But in many instances, that's just what we need to be.

I prefaced this article with my brief promotional moment on salesmanship to establish something important. I'm establishing a need—the need for project managers to act as salespeople. That's critical. But what's more critical is that I've heard the need in the first place. I've heard it from project managers around the country. I've heard it from team members who have watched their project managers founder as salespeople. I have heard a need. And listening to that need is what selling is all about.

I learned this lesson well from my brother-in-law David. He used to sell used cars. That's what he did. And he did it remarkably well. David would move twenty-three units a month. For those of you uninitiated in the auto industry, that's roughly a car a day. That's a Herculean effort. It's an amazing achievement. Particularly when you're trying to sell month after month and year after year, it's hard to maintain that kind of pace. But David was king of the salespeople. Why? I don't attribute it to Svengali-like powers or machismo or good looks (although David might argue). David is an average guy who wears a plaid flannel shirt very well. But he does have one trait that many of us lack: He is a master listener. He has the ability to draw out and educe information that might otherwise be missed. He does what we, as project managers, should do and do well: listen to what the customer, our team members, and our management need. He has the ability to listen to what people are saying, iterate their needs from those statements, and identify the means to fill those voids. It's a gift. It's a talent. It's something we can gain a valuable lesson from.

I say this because I have attempted to emulate his listening skills on a number of occasions. When I am tempted to talk to fill a conversational void, I ardently try to shut myself up. When I sense someone is foundering for words, I strive *not* to fill the void with my perception of what they're trying to say. When someone says, "I don't think I know," I send them back to the well one more time to try to come up with a response. It makes a change in their behaviors as well as mine. The more I find myself listening, the more I find the other parties sharing valuable information. The more I find myself listening, the more I find that I feel truly connected with the people I'm working with. The more I find myself listening, the more I find myself able to identify with them and identify with their needs. And *that* is what project management is all about. It's about identifying needs and working to serve those needs.

If we are to truly sell project management, either internally or externally, we must first master a small component of the art of sales itself. Listen to those around us as they identify the needs the project was intended to address. Those needs are not expressed solely in the requirements. They are expressed in every conversation we have with client management, with our management, and with the team. And as we ferret out these supplemental insights and needs, if we document them, we get a secondary bonus. They are now captured for the rest of the team and for project posterity. We become not only salespeople but also pioneers leading the organization toward its project future.

* * *

New Year's Project Resolutions: Five New Tactics and Tools to Try in the Year Ahead

Setting the Stage for Project Efficacy Ahead

(January 2003)

The new year is well underway, and, by now, many of us have already broken our New Year's resolutions. I might suggest that the new year is a great excuse to drag out some new strategies for project implementation. Oddly enough, folks in many organizations seem ready and willing to accept changes at the beginning of the year that they would otherwise be unwilling to consider. Take advantage of this "accepting" mentality and put it to work to your advantage. Specifically, here are five strategies, tactics, and tools you may wish to consider as a means to enhance practice in your organization. Some are tried and true. Others are bleeding edge and relatively untested. In both cases, they represent a chance to examine the way your organization does business.

Resolution 1: I will be the king/queen of the templates. Okay, template construction is boring. Dull. Dull. Dull. But templates ensure consistency. They affirm some uniformity can and will be applied in the organization. They affirm what's important and what's not. They identify what information is critical and how it should be retained. The key to success in a template is to be able to point to where it has been applied successfully and to clarify how and where it will be applied.

Samples of well-crafted and well-applied templates go a long way toward ensuring their proper application later on.

Resolution 2: I will try a cutting-edge project management tool, like David Hillson's risk breakdown structure (RBS) (Hillson 2002). At the 2002 national PMI Symposium, David Hillson presented a groundbreaking paper suggesting organizations can get a better perspective on their risks and their project issues by implementing his new risk breakdown structure (now referenced in *A Guide to the Project Management Body of Knowledge)*. Dr. Hillson is the self-proclaimed Risk Doctor, and one of my peers in the risk geek community. The risk breakdown structure is much like any of a variety of matrixes seeking to analyze project potential or concerns. With the risk breakdown structure, Hillson suggests organizations can increase their understanding of their risk factors and the effect they're having on a given project by creating a standardized list of risk factors and creating a simple matrix with the lowest level of the work breakdown structure (WBS). For each task in the WBS, the individual applying the RBS will evaluate it against each of the risk factors, simply to determine whether those risk factors are potentially present within the activity. The result is a matrix populated with a cross-reference of risks and work packages. Those work packages with the highest number of potential risk factors are seen as the highest risk activities. Those risk factors with the highest number of activities are seen as the highest risk factors within the project. As simple as it may sound, the insight provided is another tool in the battle to identify the big-issue risks on a project, either from the task- or risk-area perspective.

Resolution 3: I will find new applications of the software tools. Perhaps the greatest tragedy in applying software tools is that many users don't understand the breadth of the capabilities that exist, shortchanging the users from their full potential. Whether the tool is Primavera or Microsoft

Project, there are myriad capabilities most organizations either don't fully understand or exercise. Tied to Resolution 1, it's possible now to build templates within the software packages. Microsoft Project, for example, has thirty text fields and a similar number of numbers fields for project managers to apply in spreadsheets at their discretion. If that's not sufficiently advanced, consider a foray into some of the new software packages and iterations, such as the newly updated (and now for-profit) Risk Radar, available through www.spmn.com. No matter the choice, find out what you may have been missing in applying the tools.

Resolution 4: I will invest real time with a team member. When I say real time, I refer to another article, "It's a Beautiful Day in the (Project) Neighborhood." Select any team member or stakeholder from the customer to an internal team member to a vendor, and the next time she calls or stops by your office, take the time to clear out the other distractions before beginning the conversation. Shut down the computer screen, and mute the phone (or put it on do not disturb). Isolate the time you invest with her as purely time with her, excluding all the other potential distractions. Such time is eerily effective. It draws people into a more efficacious conversation and ensures a heightened sense of clarity on both sides of the discussion.

Resolution 5: I will find a new means to transfer knowledge. *Knowledge management* is a hot buzz phrase in project management, and project managers who find new and effective ways to share insights and information will continue to lead the practice. Whether it is something as pedantic as building a lessons-learned database or as clever as NASA's WebToons (*www.nas.**nasa**.gov/News/Techreports/1998/ PDF/nas-98-014.pdf*), the key to success will be infusing the means and methods to enable real input into the repository of information and—in many ways, more important—extracting it back out. Without the transfer of knowledge within an organization, the organization is only as good or effective as its current cadre of experts. The organizations that find the means to build on their expertise over time have a clear winning edge.

None of these practices, in and of themselves, are necessarily going to be considered radical. But because they may represent a shift from current practice or from historical precedent, they may draw attention. Good. That's part of the idea. A key to success in building a practice is to find out what people like and dislike about it.

One final analogy. About three years ago, I stood at the cutting edge as I bought the first new car I ever owned in my life. I purchased one of Daimler–Chrysler's PT Cruisers. I put in my order the first day the dealerships accepted orders and was the first owner on the block for the better part of six months (while others waited through the backlog). I was a Cruiser pioneer. About a week after I got my car, I drove through the Burger King drive-through window for a soda. The young man at the window stood agape at my vehicle.

"This is one of those … those … uh …"

"It's a PT Cruiser," I proudly replied.

"I saw these in a car magazine," he offered excitedly. "I hate them."

Oddly enough, that didn't bother me. But it did energize me. I realized I had incited some passion over something that for most of my life had been perceived as an unexciting element of who I was and what I did. My car had gone from being an adjunct to being an accent!

As the new year rolls along, we have that same opportunity as project managers. We can pioneer something that may prove to be popular (or loathed), and we can do so with relative impunity. We have the beauty of being able to blame it on the time of year. It's a chance to infuse some new capacities and capabilities into our PM practices. Happy New Year!

* * *

Building Management Support for Project Management

Getting True Support and Sponsorship from the Upper Echelons

(April 2003)

One visitor to www.projectconnections.com sent an e-mail asking for help in building management support for project management after the PM practice's primary champion passed away. She asked how to get management to understand the need for project management. It's a question many of us ask.

I suggest we can never convince people of the need for project management if they don't convince themselves. Getting them to convince themselves, however, is a journey we can readily help them take. Think about a telemarketer you actually spoke with in the past year. What did it take to get you to stop and listen to that presentation? That telemarketer was offering something you needed, something you could not resist.

That becomes our mission. We need to be able to offer services they cannot resist. And although such services vary widely from organization to organization, here are four basic services that may start you on your way (or facilitate your efforts if the journey has already begun):

- Communications liaison

- Charter author

- Project management software clairvoyant

- Master researcher

Communications Liaison

Most sales are actually done by providing evidence that the product or service being offered fills a need. One of the critical needs in any organization is the need for clear communication. This is normally a more dramatic need in projects than in conventional functional environments because of the nature of the difference between the two. In a conventional functional environment, the chain of command frequently becomes the model for all communications. Worker talks to supervisor, supervisor talks to manager, manager talks to executive management. The lines of command are clear and simple. There's not a lot of room for confusion. Because of that simplicity, the project environment sometimes becomes a wild mélange of information because of the nature of the environment. Because there is no clear chain of command, the relationships among the parties become fuzzy. And because they're fuzzy, the communications become fuzzy.

Our role? We can become the arbiters of quality communication. We can create the structure that builds in a modicum of clarity where it did not exist before. How? Identify the communication needs of the key players and ensure there's someone to fill those needs. Become the project archivist (or appoint one). Create subdirectories where most or all the information for the project can be found. Create regular team updates via e-mail or other sources. Orchestrate or facilitate meetings (but only if you really know how to control a crowd).

This last point is definitely a place to either win hearts or to destroy your image. In organizations where meeting control is a major issue, the ability to control meetings is a major roadblock (or opportunity to excel). Some survival tactics? Put up the schedule and agenda, and stick to it like glue. Emphasize that you'll be doing so from the start and why. Stress that it's out of respect for the time and commitment of each person in the room. If you're afraid of losing control of the time, turn it back over to the participants by establishing a protocol for violating that schedule, and make sure they have the final say on whether it's violated. Also, if there are individuals senior to you who have a propensity for dragging out discussions, invite them to send a proxy (a representative). Don't invite them or ask them in advance what it would take to control the discussion. Explain your reasons for limiting their meeting participation and your aims for the meeting in general, and make them your ally, rather than confronting them in the session. Control those individuals who often seem out of control, and you'll definitely win some hearts to project management.

Charter Author

The Project Management Institute, on the PMP certification exam, suggests that the project charter is authored by senior management. In the ideal, that may be true. In most organizations, however, the project manager writes it, if it exists at all. By designating yourself as the charter author, you become the individual who determines how the project description is couched and what management will ultimately concur is the approach to be used. That's a major responsibility. It's also a major opportunity.

It becomes a more significant opportunity with a set of signatures. One of the defining moments of my career came when I hounded a boss to the very gates of unemployment, asking for a signature. When he suggested my next request might be my last, I explained that he had fired the two project managers on the effort before me, and if he didn't sign, it would be a matter of simply postponing the inevitable for another six months. I got the signature. And that signature gave my project charter ten times the weight it would have had had I simply "run it by him." Granted, there's a level of risk associated with that type of behavior, but it creates enormous opportunity and makes the project manager the judge of what the project ultimately looks like.

How does this sell *them* on the notion of your value? You save them the time and effort of authorship. You save them the struggle to define what the project is. You're taking a load off their shoulders and acknowledging their authority at the same time.

Project Management Software Clairvoyant

Still, most managers want the authority to make changes. They feel that's their role. They need to be adjusting and tweaking and improving. We should afford them that capability. And we can make them look good in doing it, if we can actually flex some of the muscle in the project management software.

A project baseline, properly loaded into the software, will have dependencies, resources, and a host of other information embedded about the project. Some project managers try to circumvent the onus of data entry by loading in a series of fixed dates (rather than dependencies) and identifying resources at the summary level (rather than in each individual work package or task, depending upon approach). Don't! There's power in those dependencies. There's a wealth of insight provided by loading resources work package by work package. And it proves itself when we conduct those what-if analyses.

The beauty of loading the baseline properly into the PM software packages is that it becomes possible to highlight and illustrate what happens if a single resource is changed or if an activity or sequence of activities is added. It provides a crystal ball into which we can peer and make predictions about project performance, delivery dates, and potential conflicts among the functions. To do this well, we need to either get the information from management in advance to present the insights and the alternatives or become the resident whiz kid on the project management software. That's a real challenge.

As PM software becomes progressively more complex (and even the low-end tools are becoming just that), the learning curve on clairvoyance is climbing. But if management has a propensity for change, it may be worth the investment to serve as the strongest link in the chain in understanding the tools.

By becoming facile in the tools, we again provide management with a valuable service it might not have believed was available or have understood it could flex.

Master Researcher

There is a lot we don't know. There is a lot our management doesn't know. There's a significant information gap, and we have the opportunity to fill some small part of it. Hot topics in project management? Communications. Critical chain. *Good to Great* by Jim Collins (Collins 2001). Extreme PM. Portfolio. The Project Management Office (PMO). Risk. Each of these topics has its masters. Each has its latest writings and readings. Each has some new nuance or flavor to enhance the way we do business. As project managers, we can help our management shop the market of ideas.

The www.projectconnections.com Web site has a lot of information in these areas. There are a lot of great texts out there to read and review. There's a wealth of insight and a mountain of opportunities to extract it. My commitment? Read ten pages a day. Ten pages of just about anything. But I must read ten pages a day. Why? I then commit myself to sharing what I've learned in my next presentation, meeting, or discussion. And by channeling that information out, I become more valuable to those in the organizations I serve. It doesn't take much to find ten pages of content you didn't know about before. Start on the www.projectconnections. com Web site. There are hundreds of articles, templates, and other content. Check out the latest issues of *Project Manager Today* (www.pmtoday.co.uk) or PMNetwork (www.pmi.org), or just do a search on project management on www.amazon. com. By becoming a voracious reader, you become a greater asset to your organization and to your management.

Going for the Close

Finally, affirm to management the value you're bringing on a regular basis. It's not well advised to simply take these actions and assume they'll acknowledge them. They may not. Instead, if we're going to take these actions, we need to ensure we present them for what they are. They are value-added and need to be valued as such. We need to trumpet them as accomplishments and as steps forward for the organization as a whole. And if we are able to make those accomplishments sufficiently visible, we will, with luck, leave management wanting for more and wondering what other information we may have at our disposal. Twisting the Edward Fitzgerald quote from *The Rubáiyát of Omar Khayyám* (Fitzgerald 1995), "I wonder often what the [project managers] buy one half so precious as the stuff they sell." Let's leave our management with that sentiment.

* * *

Exploring Project Management

Looking for New Ideas as We Start New Projects

(June 2003)

From *Chambers Dictionary of Etymology* (Barnhart 1999): Explore *v.* "1585, in letters of Queen Elizabeth I ... in some instances, a direct borrowing from Latin *explorare* ... originally said to be a hunters' term meaning to set up a loud cry to scare an animal from its hiding place, but later changed to mean beat the bushes."

Project managers as explorers—it's an interesting concept. I had the honor of sitting in for Dr. Young Hoon Kwak at George Washington University recently, and as I arrived for class, the students were turning in their midterm examinations for risk management. Dr. Kwak is an educator at GWU, and is a long-standing figure in the project risk management community. Seizing the opportunity, I looked at a few of the exams and reflected on my college days as a journalism major at The Ohio State University. It struck me how far the profession had come in a quarter century. In 1978, no university offered a master's in project management. Now, dozens do. And more are added every year. In the late '70s, people didn't think in terms of project management as a career path by itself. Now it's evolving that way. This means a sea change in the way project managers evolve professionally. Rather than being thrust into completely unfamiliar territory, the new project managers have some grounding. They have an understanding of what they're in for. They know what to expect. They know what a Gantt chart is before they're asked to present one for the first time. They have a sense of what team building is supposed to be and how a communications plan is deployed. Twenty-five years ago, project managers were on a voyage of self-discovery, and, in the process, they were setting down practices that have now become commonplace.

Explorers and Pioneers

It's not unlike the difference between the pioneers and settlers. Pioneers are the first to tread into unfamiliar turf. They find the paths that work and suffer through those that don't. Some don't make it to safe ground. Pioneers are the first in their country or organization to set down the rules and name the terms. "We will call this state 'Nevada'." Or in the project management sense, "When we say 'risk plan,' this is what we mean." In the late '70s, the terms were still being defined. Now, the maps have been drawn, and we're working toward common definitions, terms, and routes. That's not to say there's not still plenty of areas in project management ripe for exploration, but the major paths for the uninitiated have been carved out, tramped down, and paved.

Those coming through now still have a chance to do some exploration. Not necessarily in terms of setting down the terms and terminology but, instead, for the more classic definition of *explore* as that found in the *Chambers* text cited earlier: "To scare animals from their hiding places." Project managers get to raise the alarm. They get to warn, alarm, and alert. They get to flush out the last vestiges of antiquated practice and move project management toward a recognizable, consistent profession. As they do so, there are explorers' tools, just as there have always been—but now they take on a different look and feel.

Explorers' Tools

The tools we use to "frighten" the last vestiges of aging practices away are not the same tools (Gantt, network diagram, responsibility matrix, etc.) used to implement project management. If we want to make project management habitable and inviting, the tools to deploy are those that ensure best practice takes hold. Here are three examples:

ISO 10006: The basic quality guidance on project management from the International Organization for Standardization provides a benchmark as to what protocols to follow. It doesn't spell out the specific paths or methodologies, but it tells what signs are out there to indicate best-practice project management. Keep watching in the years ahead, as ISO presents its own project management standard.

Taxonomy-Based Risk Identification (Carr et al. 1993)*:* This monstrous list of risk questions on the Software Engineering Institute's Web site (www.sei.cmu.edu) is a classic example of taking advantage of the insights others have gained blazing a trail. And because the list of questions highlights past experience, there's evidence of potential gain from its use.

A Guide to the Project Management Body of Knowledge: PMI's landmark work spells out terms, definitions, and guidance as it has developed over the past few decades. As with the other tools, it is highly regarded not because of its specificity but because of its widespread acceptance from organization to organization and industry to industry.

What makes these tools work? They work because we can point to them, outside our organization, and say it is time for change. We can use them to highlight the fact that others are blazing the same trails in different cultures, organizations, and industries. We can use them to show there is a path ahead worth treading, and if we don't clear the brush of the ad hoc practices, we will be left behind by the settlers who are willing to trace the paths pioneers and explorers established.

Back Where We Started

T. S. Eliot, in "Little Gidding," captures one last interesting notion:

We shall not cease from exploration
And the end of all our exploring
Will be to arrive where we started
And know the place for the first time.

In project management, we find ourselves repeating similar projects, reliving similar experiences, and encountering similar challenges day to day and year to year. Twenty-five years ago, each time it happened was a fresh opportunity to blaze the trail. Today, we start afresh at the beginning of the project road, but armed with new tools and insights, we have the opportunity to make the trip more smoothly, more efficiently, and more skillfully than the project explorers ever could.

* * *

My Vacation's Through and So Is My Creativity

Ten Ideas on How to Come Up with Ten Ideas for Your Next Project—Waxing Creative!

(September 2003)

September. Back to school. Back to work. Back to the grindstone. And the eerie thing is that management actually expects you to be revived, regenerated, and recuperated after an exhausting week or two at the (insert your favorite vacation spot here). And so it goes. Management wants you to develop project plans. Risk lists. Customer solutions. Dynamic briefings. "Oh, and make sure it's creative, please."

That can be a tall order. Creativity does not exactly pour from every pore when you're still trying to recover from your rest and relaxation. But there are some ways to come up with something exciting, new, and different. Consider these ten simple strategies.

Strategy 1: Dust off the dusty archive: Virtually every project manager has a personal version of the dusty archive. It's old plans, documentation, and memos you've meant to sort through or throw away but haven't quite sifted through yet. What a resource! It not only revives old ideas and approaches in a new light but also helps solve the what-should-I-throw-away syndrome. And in the process of sifting for new ideas, you get some housekeeping out of the way.

Strategy 2: Consider a career change: You're no longer a construction engineer/software developer/oil rig designer/utility designer; now you're a baker/painter/powerful corporate mogul. How would your perspective on your creative needs change? It's not your design project anymore; it's a fourteen-tier wedding cake. It's not your plant shutdown anymore; it's a staff reorganization. What would their perspective be on the problem you're trying to solve? How would they approach it? If nothing else, it serves as affirmation of why you chose the career you chose.

Strategy 3: Conduct a web search: Can you boil down to two or three words your issue/concern/problem/creative nuisance? The Web has an amazing way of turning up the wrong answers. That's fine. Sometimes, in the creative flow, the wrong answers have the capacity to open our eyes to new solutions. Don't forget that most search engines have the ability to look only within the .gov or .org domains, and Web sites like www.projectconnections.com have internal search engines.

Strategy 4: Resolve to absorb fifteen minutes of silence: Fifteen minutes in isolation. Away from your computer, cell phone, and all other electronics. Just you, a piece of paper, and the thrust of your latest dilemma scrawled across the top of the paper. Take a walk out of your normal environs to the nearest reasonably quiet spot. Libraries, hotel lobbies, parks, or even your own car (radio off, thanks) in the parking deck can provide a momentary haven from all outside distractions. And that may be all it takes to start the creative energy flowing.

Strategy 5: Read the New York Times Business Bestsellers List: Granted, not as quick a strategy as the others, but a most effective one nonetheless. Business books have a lot of wonderful ideas that can be boiled down to the project level. Recent hits like *Good to Great: Why Some Companies Make the Leap ... and Others Don't* (Collins 2001), and *Execution: The Discipline of Getting Things Done* (Bossidy and Charan 2002) share analogy after analogy that can find its way into your ideation process. (It also makes you look downright erudite.)

Strategy 6: Use them: Maybe you're not the creative force for this particular effort. Use them. "Them" would be the people you work with, serve, or partner with. Send out an e-mail asking for one thought, one nudge, one risk, one design element, one *anything*. That's the key. Ask for help, and little will happen. Ask for a whole design, and you'll hear less. But ask for one narrow, specific *something* and you're sure to get a response. (And if you get two, they're being generous.)

Strategy 7: Peruse Brewer's Dictionary of Phrase and Fable (Ayto 2006): Wow! You're completely tapped out. You have nothing left to talk about, to include, to share, or from which to draw an analogy. Your next presentation is looking like a visit from The Bore. You can't think of a single new anecdote. *Brewer's* to the rescue! Warning: This tome is addictive. Look up a catchphrase, term, or word, and find some new fascinating factoid. From "A1" (derived from Lloyd's of London's classification of ship's hull conditions) to "zany" (derived from the Italian *zanni*, meaning "buffoon," but which became a nickname for Giovanni/John), it's an epic experience.

Strategy 8: Don the hats: Put on another "hat." Don't think like yourself. Pretend you're the executive down the hall. Or the customer on the other end of the help line. Or the recipient of whatever you're delivering. What would you want then? What would you expect? Keep changing characters. You'll come up with something.

Strategy 9: Take a picture (it lasts longer): With a digital camera, you're empowered. Create your own story around virtually any office photo. Create mental captions for them. It ties to "The Hats" earlier, but it adds some focus. The clarity brought out by a picture of someone slumped over a computer or two team members having a hall chat can be surprising.

Strategy 10: Poof! Make someone a guinea pig: Who just walked into your cube? A team member? Maintenance? Security? It doesn't matter. That person just became the resident resource for new ideas. He's a prisoner. And you own him. Block the door. Barricade him in your office until he shares his perspective on your problem. Great ideas come from some surprising resources.

You don't have to wait until you're desperate to try new techniques to extract ideas. Try them before you get desperate. Try them while you're still fresh, and they'll have even higher yield. Even if coming up with new ideas has never been a problem, different techniques can generate some interesting and different results.

* * *

Project Managing Up: Getting Management Buy-in to Project Management

Looking at Ways to Get Management to Share Our Collective Visions

(March 2004)

You've arrived. Your team understands the basics of project management. You have a certification. You have the software. All seems right with the world. Just one problem: Management still sees you as potentially unnecessary overhead. At best, you are an administrative nuisance that the customer demands. At worst, you're a hindrance to the sales department. Your mission? Get management to see the value of project management.

This has been and continues to be a quandary for project managers for years. For many of us in the profession, our own families have trouble understanding what we do for a living, let alone the management teams above us. For some, the answer has been to host presentations on the goals and objectives of project management. For others, the answer has been to shift the job into an amalgam of technical performance and project management commitments.

If we really want management buy-in to what we're doing, we need to get back to the classic question of what's in it for them. That's a question senior management asks, and we should be ready to answer. But the answer is not that we'll provide reports, updates, and efficient use of resources (although we'll definitely do that, as well). The answer is that we give management the ability to manage. We open the door so management can make informed decisions. We give management options.

One of the classic complaints of managers at all levels is that they don't get to do as much managing as they would like. They express concern that they spend their time in administration rather than management. Moving paper around versus making decisions. Which would you rather do?

We can afford our managers the opportunity to do more of the latter by educating them on what we can provide. But that then means they actually have to understand project management, which is a bridge some managers are not quite prepared to cross. To get them over, we need to become the educators. But rather than teaching them network diagramming or team dynamics in the project environment, we should be teaching them what options they have to manage us. And, by virtue of the backdoor relationship between the two, they'll probably learn a lot about project management in the process.

What Can Your Managers Expect?

Managers don't know your capabilities. They are frequently unaware that they should expect clear, unambiguous scope statements. They often don't know that the project manager should have a baseline schedule and cost plan and should be able to identify variance from that plan. They don't know that relative levels of resource consumption should be tracked and identifiable.

Rather than teaching them these practices, consider

teaching your management the questions you (as a project manager) are capable of answering:

- Do we have a clear, mutually agreed-upon synopsis of what the customer wants?

- Has there been any change to that synopsis since last we met?

- How much work have we done?

- How does that compare to how much work was to be done by now?

- How much did we spend on it?

- How does that compare to how much we were to have spent for that work?

- Do you need any support from me to get it back on track?*

- What risks (if any) need to be escalated to my level?*

- Did any of our major risks turn into realities?

- What changes have been made to the project?

- Is the customer happy?

- Are the team members satisfied with their work?

- Do you need any of my intervention with the customer or the team?*

Note that the questions with asterisks (*) are the actual management intervention questions. They are where management works to earn a salary. The rest of the questions are so that they can put those asterisked questions in the proper context. Frequently, executives I've worked with have been unaware that their project managers should have this depth of information at their disposal on an ongoing basis. This is not special information that should just have to be churned out for a special management meeting. It's information that should be embedded in the project plans and available at virtually a moment's notice.

It's a an impressive set of information, but if the senior management team doesn't know it's out there, the team can't act on it. It's not asking senior managers to micromanage. It's asking them to take on a role appropriate to their level and responsibility.

What the Questions Teach Them

I used to drive junk. As a result, I had an extended relationship with my mechanic and the staff at Donald B. Rice Tire Company (my mechanic), the home of "round tires and square deals." I used to take an uninformed management position in dealing with them. "Here's my car. It's broken. Fix it." And they would. But the relationship was sometimes contentious. I was uncomfortable with their determining what would happen to my car (and my wallet). That's not unlike the approach some executives take with projects. "Here's the customer and the project. Do what he wants. Make him happy." And the executives become uncomfortable because they are uncertain of what's happening to their customer (and their wallet).

In time, through the careful, guided coaching of a few true professionals, I learned to ask the mechanic the right questions. What parts will you be replacing? Are there alternative approaches (junk parts, refurbished parts)? Is there anything else I might want to address while you have that part off the car? In the process, I felt more in control. I was able to make more decisions (although I still have no clue how to do what my mechanic does). I was a more informed customer of their services. I learned to do this because a few professionals took the time to say, "If you want more control, here are the questions to ask."

Knowing the questions opens the door for a clearer understanding and a greater sense of management control. I have no idea how to replace a water pump, but I now know that they can be purchased refurbished or new (and that you rarely want to strip one off a car in the junkyard). I have options. The options all work for my mechanic because I'm not changing the work he does. I am changing my perceived level of control.

In trying to teach management the project management questions, project managers sometimes feel compelled to teach Auto Mechanics 101. That's a mistake. Management doesn't need to know *how* to build a network diagram. Senior managers do need to know that their project managers know how to sequence activities and can identify, at a glance, when the activities will cascade one into the next to extend the schedule too far. And if there are alternative ways to arrange the schedule, then management should be aware of the alternatives and their implications, without having to learn the intricacies of the finish–finish or start–start relationship.

Getting Management to the Right Questions

To get management there, we can start by laying out the options. Consider these two approaches:

- The team is in the storming phase of Tuckman's model of group development (Tuckman 1965), and some intervention on your part would help move them to norming.

- There's some team contention over roles and responsibilities, and I'd appreciate some help. If you could either sign off on the responsibilities list for the functional managers or consider giving us some war room space down on the fourth floor, it would actually help a lot in terms of minimizing some of the conflict we have going on right now.

The first is probably a more in-depth explanation of the rationale for why the help is needed, but it is also a weaker approach because it forces management to understand some of the nuances that it, frankly, shouldn't have to. Tuckman's model may be a nice piece of data for them to have, but it really doesn't address what senior management is expected to do. They don't have time to learn the implications of forming, storming, norming, and performing.

The second operates from the notion that senior managers will ask the right questions if they're given the right data. The more we can do to outline those options for them, to engage them in the options within their sphere of control, and to afford them the opportunity to manage, the more we will see them participating at appropriate levels and supporting the project organization. Ultimately, they'll be a lot happier with their mechanics.

* * *

Another Day in Paradise: Life in Projectland

Sometimes It's All About Your Attitude

(April 2007)

Those who know me and who have worked with me in the past, know the familiar title of this article. I'm often asked, "How's it going?" My response? "It's another day in paradise." Is it? Not always. Then again, it beats the heck out of the alternatives.

Think about the current state of your project and your project organization. Are they perfect? I seriously doubt that many of you actually answered yes. But, do they represent the opportunity for significant improvement or change or continued employment? For at least one of those, I would hope the answer is yes. The key to embracing your project as another day in paradise, I contend, is to redefine paradise.

When I was still in college, I was a fry cook at a local sit-down restaurant. This was not a fancy establishment, just a local eatery. Around me were many middle-aged and older women, including one I'll call Shirley. Shirley was the eternal optimist, ever ready with a smile or kind word. On your worst day, it was difficult not to smile back at Shirley. She had worked at the restaurant for years before I got there and probably worked there for years thereafter. There were no hopes of stock options, major advancement, or breakthrough opportunities. How did she keep that attitude? A major part of it was recognizing that she had a willingness (and in some ways, it seemed a personal obligation) to define paradise down to the current levels and to get others to enjoy the trip.

The Paradise Mind-set

I had several near-cathartic events yesterday. On the eve of a flight out for a major long-distance trip, my computer began flashing the "blue screen of death." As we all know, that's never a good thing. The trick is to know how bad it is. On many days, I would have spent much of the day popping a blood vessel while waiting for and dealing with the help desk. Although it took a full twelve hours, five technicians, and three major multinational corporations to resolve the problem, I maintained much greater composure than I had in years. I did so specifically because I had hope, based on two factors:

- I developed a game plan for where the effort would wind up if everything continued to go wrong.

- In twenty-four hours from the time the disaster started, I was leaving for Hawaii with my lovely wife.

Okay, I confess. The latter actually probably had more influence than I give it credit for, but even so, it was actually the *source* of the pain as well. I had to have a running laptop for the business opportunity on Oahu, so I was between the proverbial rock and hard place. With that going on, I still wasn't freaking out for one simple reason—hope.

Hope is amazing. It ties into the expectancy theory by Victor Vroom of the Yale School of Management (Vroom 1964). Vroom posits that if we believe an effort will bring with it a positive outcome, we will work harder and have a higher level of motivation associated with that effort. Knowing that I would, no matter what, have to be on a plane in less than twenty-four hours led me to the strange belief that I would somehow have a resolution in that time. It also helped to keep me from losing my cool when professionals were expressing their belief that the system might have to be sacrificed to the computer gods.

There are multiple ways we can leverage this to our advantage on projects. The first is to remind ourselves and our team members that if we develop a viable set of alternative solutions, paradise is still a potential outcome. Part of that is to affirm what constitutes paradise. It may be just a state of survival without doing harm to the status quo. Part of it may be an opportunity to make even the tiniest of inroads on a much larger problem. Part of it may simply be a clear understanding that the goal, however distant, is ultimately worthwhile.

What is paradise today? Define it. Clearly state it. Paradise might be defined as any situation that is not doing harm to us and affords an opportunity for growth. It might be defined as the absence of pain. Oddly enough, organizations often seem committed to defining hell long before they ever get around to defining heaven. Team members and project managers alike often seem committed to the Nietzschean paradigm of "that which does not kill me makes me stronger." They would rather define all that's wrong in an organization rather than what's right.

The reality should be just the opposite: That which affords me *hope* makes me stronger. In a project environment, if we wish to engender hope, we need to cite the opportunities that exist in every work package and in every approach we identify. When disasters befall us (even as limited as my computer meltdown), we need to identify where the optimistic elements may reside. In some cases, the mere notion that we have a proposed route for survival is enough to qualify as paradise. The potential absence of suffering stands as an improvement over where we might otherwise be.

Project managers hold a unique position in their ability to drive individuals to a shared posture of optimism. They get there, however, by emphasizing the aspects of paradise in which the project is evolving. The more we can do to affirm that optimism and direct others to identify the alternatives that may potentially minimize any pain and angst, the further down the road to paradise we find ourselves.

At 8:15 p.m. last night (Eastern time), I hung up the phone with the last technician. In the last fifteen minutes of effort, we had rectified the problem on my primary laptop *and* had finished reconditioning my backup laptop to the point where both could serve the need for the upcoming trip. It is now 4:25 p.m. (Hawaii time). My wife and I are at 34,000 feet and about three hours out from the Aloha State, where I don't have to show up for work for three days.

It's another day in paradise.

* * *

The Hierarchy of Holiday Stakeholders

Establishing a Taxonomy/Breakdown of Stakeholders as a New Way to Look at the Body of Folks We Deal With

(December 2007)

No matter the religion or belief system, between now and the first weeks of the new year, most of us will savor the joy of rekindled friendships, a shared repast, and a celebration or two. But will we have actually considered all the people we need to consider?

Stakeholder identification is a challenge of project management and a challenge in virtually any environment. The beauty of holiday gatherings is that they provide both a common frame of reference and a common metaphor for taking a new look at a practice we all strive to achieve: effective stakeholder identification.

Most efforts in this area are amorphous, allowing for brainstorms or freewheeling identification practices to, we hope, catch the full body of stakeholders. Watching this happen time and again, I came to realize that although we have breakdown structures and taxonomies for organizations, contracts, risk, resources, work, and virtually everything else in project management, there is no taxonomy of stakeholders. And although we could readily tie stakeholder analysis to one of the other breakdown structures, the nature of stakeholders is sufficiently consistent that a common taxonomy may be applicable. Such a taxonomy, in a formal setting, might look like this:

1.0 Internal

    1.1 Department

        1.1.1 Management

        1.1.2 Team

        1.1.3 Nonteam Users

        1.1.4 Nonteam Nonusers

    1.2 Department

        1.2.1 Management

        1.2.2 Team

        1.2.3 Nonteam Users

        1.2.4 Nonteam Nonusers

    1.3 Accounting

        1.3.1 Management ...

    1.4 Finance

        1.4.1 Management ...

    1.5 Legal

        1.5.1 Management ...

1.6 Project

    1.6.1 Management …

2.0 External

    2.1 Vendor

        2.1.1 Management

        2.1.2 Team

        2.1.3 Sales

        2.1.4 Support

        2.1.5 Contracts

    2.2 Client

        2.2.1 Management

        2.2.2 Team

        2.2.3 Support

        2.2.4 Contracts

    2.3 Nonclient External

        2.3.1 Management

        2.3.2 Connecting Forces

        2.3.3 Influence Groups and Committees

    2.4 Government and Regulatory

        2.4.1 Management

        2.4.2 Oversight

        2.4.3 Support

Although this taxonomy seems rather sterile (and it is), when you put it in the context of your next holiday gathering/

party/fete, it puts a little clarifying meat on the bones. Just going through the exercise of trying to find stakeholders in each category goes a long way toward being able to put faces with the titles and people in the roles to participate as active stakeholders.

1.0 Internal

   1.1 Department 1 (our family)

      1.1.1 Management (my wife)

      1.1.2 Team (my sons)

      1.1.3 Nonteam Users (my sons' invited friends)

      1.1.4 Nonteam Nonusers (my sons' uninvited friends who still want to be able to use the basement to practice with their rock band with the volume set to 11)

   1.2 Department 2 (my in-laws)

      1.2.1 Management (my mother-in-law)

      1.2.2 Team (my brother- and sister-in-law)

      1.2.3 Nonteam Users (their families)

      1.2.4 Nonteam Nonusers (the legion of cousins we didn't invite who, if they find out that we're having this little gathering, will probably turn on us when Thanksgiving rolls around next year)

   1.3 Accounting (my wife) (Hey, Carl! You already said your wife! I know I did, but she's also a CPA, and I'm not about to put someone else in this role. Besides, she has different stakes in this role than when she's running family gatherings.)

> 1.3.1 Management (my wife)
>
> 1.3.2 Team (me, as one of the primary breadwinners in the household)
>
> 1.3.3 Nonteam Users (those who will also tap my wallet)
>
> 1.3.4 Nonteam Nonusers (those who do not get a shot at my holiday largesse)

1.4 Legal (okay, not every category applies on *every* project)

1.5 Project

> 1.5.1 Management (the cook, which would be me again, but in a different role)
>
> 1.5.2 Team (the logistics team, which would be my wife and sons again, but in different roles)
>
> 1.5.3 Nonteam Users (the in-laws again, but this time as consumers)
>
> 1.5.4 Nonteam Nonusers (the cousins again, this time when they find out they missed basket after basket of home-baked bread)

2.0 External

2.1 Vendor (the grocery store)

> 2.1.1 Management (Believe it or not,

some of us still have relationships with our local grocers. I'm notorious at my market as "The Guy with Two Carts." They love me.)

2.1.2 Team (the guy out front who gets my carts; the woman I chat with in the noodle aisle every week)

2.1.3 Sales (the deli staff; the seafood staff the meat man.)

2.1.4 Support (the cashier; the fellow who helps cram all this into my sedan)

2.1.5 Contracts (the front service desk folks who arbitrate the scanner disputes, coupon missteps, and other common market nuisances)

2.2 Client

2.2.1 Management (the neighbors who will join us)

2.2.2 Team (their kids)

2.2.3 Support (their babysitters)

2.2.4 Contracts (the person in their house responsible for the RSVP)

2.3 Nonclient External

2.3.1 Management (the neighbors who won't join us, but who will see all the cars out front and know that we're having a major "do" that they weren't invited to, causing a potential rift in neighbor-to-neighbor relations)

2.3.2 Connecting Forces (the neighbors who will incite the neighbors who weren't invited but didn't see it as a slight until the other neighbor brought up how surprised they were that *they* didn't get invited, particularly given their proximity to our home)

2.3.3 Influence Groups and Committees (The Neighborhood Watch, who will do everything except identify the vehicle that clips the side mirror of my son's Volvo because it was parked on the street instead of the driveway)

2.4 Government and Regulatory

2.4.1 Management (You could look at this one in a variety of ways, but I see this primarily as the local constabulary or gendarmerie who have found my son's friends practicing guitar in the garage at 11 at night with the volume set to 11.)

2.4.2 Oversight (All the agencies that regulate the food we eat, the air we breathe, and the water we drink. This probably explains why we don't drink a lot of straight water during the holiday season. Everyone knows these folks take holidays too.)

2.4.3 Support (the local cab company ho picks up folks who really shouldn't be hopping in their cars to get home)

Although the names may change from project to project, at this slightly higher level, there's actually a chance we may be able to leverage our history, our experiences, and our ability to put faces to names. By doing so, we develop more comprehensive and thoughtful lists of the players we should have under consideration.

The beauty of doing this dance is that we now have the ability to identify the stakes of all the players and fantasize and plot about how they may ultimately subvert the project. If we don't work from a consistent structure, we run the risk of finding out that, in the end, we didn't meet all the needs of the critical stakeholders. At an even more rudimentary level, it clarifies for us who's "in the pool," which may be enough to ensure against subversion of our project (and holiday?) goals.

Happy Holidays to *all* my stakeholders!

* * *

The Two Toughest Letters in the Project Management Vocabulary: *N-O*

From Beginning to End, It Becomes Crucial to Get Others to Know That We Know How to Say It

(May 2008)

For project managers, *no* is often the toughest word in the English language to use. We often prefer the classic PM strategy of "yes, but ..." as the softer, kinder, gentler alternative. No sounds harsh. Uncooperative. It sounds reticent and recalcitrant. It sounds negative. And yet, for many of us, the time has come as professionals to set yes, but ... aside and venture into the world of no.

I say this because I note that, with increasing frequency, clients are not taking yes, but ... as an answer. No sooner do we offer a yes-we-can-do-that, but-it-costs-you-another-million response than the customer hears only the first half of the equation. They often seem far more interested in capability than cost. As a result, when we come to the table with the costs for their ventures, they balk.

One of my clients recently asked for a much higher level of review and a much higher degree of involvement in my consulting work than that to which I have become accustomed through the years. I agreed to a single review, but during that review, it became very clear that this was not to be a one-time event. The senior managers wanted more involvement in the work I have historically done. And so at the end of the first conference call, I tried a "yes, but" approach.

Yes, we can do additional reviews, but there will need to be a change in our contractual arrangements to accommodate them.

When they replied that they saw this as work under the contract, I realized it was not a "yes, but" situation. It called for clear, defined action.

No. I cannot continue to do these reviews, so we need to develop an exit strategy because I cannot provide the requisite number of reviews and still achieve my financial objectives.

The managers were flummoxed. They wanted to know why I had suddenly changed my tune. They wanted to know why I was willing to walk away from such a critical opportunity. They wanted to know why we should terminate a long-standing agreement over such a minor issue. I explained that I had attempted to provide reasonable accommodation, but that it was no longer possible to make the required margins with the additional reporting pressure.

They grumbled. They groused. They threatened to walk away from the contract. And then they ceded the point and went back to the original levels of tracking and reporting.

At first, the post-event relationship seemed strained and tenuous. But I think the reality is that I was projecting that on them. In fact, because I said no only once, they have actually been more cooperative, more supportive, and more sensitive to my organizational needs. And I'm the consultant!

The reality is that any business relationship is a two-way street. We have the opportunity to generate support from our clients, but in many cases, we will be able to achieve that support only if we set clear boundaries.

A Guide to the Project Management Body of Knowledge, 3rd Edition, added the term *project boundaries,* (which changed to "project exclusions" in the 4th edition) to be defined as (paraphrased) "what the project is *not.*" The fact that PMI recognized the need to define what projects are not should set off alarm bells for us as project managers while we attempt to define what our work is.

Try it. Today, identify three things that are not part of what your work is supposed to entail but that seem to find a way to creep into your day-to-day life. (No, you can't include e-mail in that list because someone has to keep up with it.) But as you identify those elements that really don't belong in your work, your daily performance, or in your relationship with the client, take a moment to ask yourself how you will deal with them the next time they rear their ugly heads.

What will I say if the client says ...?

Then practice how you will say no. Feel free to start with a yes, but ... or two, but recognize that if the client isn't willing to accept or acknowledge your but premise, then you will, ultimately, have to resort to no.

No, I cannot do that because it exceeds my capability/ mandate/contract/allowances /contingency. I prize you in this relationship, but that's outside where I can go here.

Then, after you've rehearsed it three or four times, give it a whirl. When the situation is right, take Nancy Reagan's advice from the 1980s and just say no.

Expect the firestorm. Expect challenges. Expect an unwillingness to concur that no is one of the options from the answer menu.

But if the request is genuinely beyond what your or your organization can deal with, you have just taken the first step toward a healthier relationship.

And if the client walks away?

If the request was genuinely unreasonable and would have led to bad business practice or behavior on your part, you have done your organization a positive service. Some clients (or some elements of their work) deserve to be let go. But be sure the climate is right. If you have the ability and the authority to let the client go, and if what the client is doing is not in your organizations' best interests, then you are one step closer to a healthier, stronger, and more nimble organization, and you are freeing resources to do more valued and valuable work.

Do we want to do this often? Probably not. But do we have to do this often? Definitely not. In most corporate environments, very few clients really tax an organization and its personnel to their limits. But those who do tax organizations hard do incalculable damage—damage that gets worse and costs us more the longer they're with us.

If you've set the stage well and have a clear understanding that you have the ability, the authority, and the rationale for forging ahead with a no response, it's worth a try. But remember, practice makes perfect. And if it hasn't been part of your vocabulary for a while, it might take some serious rehearsal before you're ready for the main event.

* * *

In Defense of the Project Management Perfect World

Why We Need a Perfect-World Mentality in Setting up and Implementing Our Projects

(July 2008)

One of the most common challenge questions I get when teaching Project Management Professional® exam preparation courses is why doesn't the Project Management Institute (PMI) make the test more real world? Over the years, my response to that question has evolved, but the more the question comes along, the more I realize we don't insist on the perfect world often enough.

At different times in history, there must have been pushback on any variety of steps forward in human progress. Some folks found the notion of indoor plumbing repulsive. ("You'd actually do that? In your house?") Seat belts were seen as clothes-rumpling traps that might pin us in the car in an accident. Thomas Watson when president of IBM was alleged to have said, "I think there's a world market for about five computers" (Maney 2003).

We look at a different world—a future, perfect world—because it is where the promise is. Science fiction is a popular genre in movies and books because it opens the eyes to what is possible. Since I was in my teens (quite a few years back), I've seen movies featuring flying cars. Do we have them? No. Do I hope we do some day? Sure! Is there some scientist somewhere trying to make it happen? I certainly hope so. We step into the future thanks to people who envision the world as it could be.

On the project management certification exam, many of the questions focus on an understanding of the world as it *should be* in project management. Here are a few examples:

- Senior management writes and signs chartering documents.

- Procurement departments deliver what we ask for in a timely fashion and help us craft better contracts.

- Human resources departments provide skilled resources on demand with the properly qualified skill sets.

- Management understands that range estimates are more honest and realistic than single-data-point estimates are.

Is this the world as it is? In most organizations, no. And yet, if you hope to pass the premier certification in project management, this is where you need to be. Does that make the exam wrong? No! In fact, it means that the professional association of project managers recognizes that there is, out there, as Ronald Reagan put it, "a shining city on a hill." There is an ideal. There is a standard to which we should try to hold our organizations. There can be better and more effective project management if we are willing to acknowledge that business as usual is not business as it *should* be.

Suppose the certification exam's perfect world became reality. The changes in the project management environment would be dramatic.

- Every project would have a clear business case and a defined priority within the organization.

- Resources would be respected when they provide estimates rather than forced to create padded estimates that hide reality.

- Risk contingency budgets would be overt, with clear tracking systems for when they're drawn down upon.

- There would be a consistent moment in time when project managers would answer Microsoft Project's "save with a baseline?" question in the affirmative.

In the June 4, 2008, *Washington Post,* the front page of the newspaper included an article by Dana Hedgpeth about Lockheed Martin and the Project on Government Oversight (POGO). POGO had unearthed a Defense Contract Management Agency report that cited the huge defense contractor for failing to track and manage its projects properly. The article specifically called out failings in earned value management systems (Hedgpeth 2008).

Lockheed got the attention because of the leviathan proportions of its contracts with the government. But how many smaller, leaner organizations are guilty of the same shortcomings? The argument is made that earned value and other rigid, rigorous processes of project management are too weighty. It's suggested that they're not worth the return. I doubt very much that Lockheed would agree right now. Like any organization trapped in quality shortcomings, rework is almost invariably more expensive than doing it right the first time.

Which brings us back around to PMI, the certification, and the perfect world. What good is a certification that says that every process must be followed consistently every time? It sounds good to me. It also provides a jumping-off point to take steps toward that perfect world. As more organizations demand certifications, they afford the perfect response to management seeking to shortcut the process.

Management: "Stop bothering the client with all those change orders for little stuff. We're building goodwill here!"

Certified manager: "It's part of best-practice process."

Management: "It's not best practice if it costs us a client!"

Certified manager: "If everyone is consistent, it won't."

Management: "But everyone's not consistent."

Certified manager: "You're telling them all to get certified to make them consistent. And the certification exam says we do this consistently, with the paperwork."

Granted, too many conversations like that and you wind up working on your résumé.

The point is that we need to acknowledge that PMI and the other certifying bodies are working toward an environment where we have consistent best practice. They have to test to the ideal, or else the ideal will never be achieved. In working on the team to generate the fourth edition of *A Guide to the Project Management Body of Knowledge*, I was occasionally surprised to hear arguments about real-world versus perfect-world project management within that group. As an American National Standards Institute (ANSI) standard, that book must reflect the ideal environment for project success. And that's an environment we should all strive to embrace.

* * *

Process: Planning

Getting Past the Big Event on Risk

Overcoming the Risk Elements That Seem Overwhelming

(May 2000)

Just this past week, I've been reminded on three separate occasions of the importance of clearly identifying the true risk "event" associated with projects. While I was teaching a seminar at the ProjectWorld conference in Boston, it became apparent that some students clearly grasped the importance of identifying risks so that others can interpret and understand them. Others, however, continued to label risks as simply "bad schedule" or "over cost" without tackling the true nature of what was driving them to that condition. The second occasion came as I was reviewing a case study on a project that incorporated highly personalized customer-by-customer deliverables. The risk statements were broad and global, including, "We may lose our allocated resources." For those for whom risk is a first-strike effort, that's not a great risk statement. In fact, it's generic. It could apply in virtually any situation. The third occasion came last night as I visited the local library with my son. I was reviewing a book on disasters (as any good risk manager might) and was struck by an article about the 1981 railroad crash in Mansi, India, that claimed 500 lives (Haine 1993). A friend of mine had warned me that if I visit India, I need to seriously consider transportation other than rail because of the crowds.

What do these three events have in common? They identify risk. But they don't do it well. The real test for whether a particular risk is identified well is whether it is something on which we can take action. Is there something we can do about it? Think about those three risks.

Bad Schedule

I can do something about this, but I'm not sure it's going to be effective. The wafer-like thinness of this particular risk makes it difficult to identify any focused solution. Although I can find ways to expedite the schedule (or to beg for more time), I can't effectively argue how I might solve the risk because I don't really know what it is. How do you solve a risk statement like this? Depth, depth, and more depth. "There's a distinct possibility (probability) the schedule may slip by three weeks (impact) if the customer doesn't follow the change control process." That's a better risk statement. It gives me the impact, the probability, and the specifics. It gives me something to manage.

We May Lose Our Allocated Resources

Once again, depth is going to help, but here, we don't even know the bad thing that will happen to us. Instead, "We may lose Phillip and, as a result, fall behind on the code" gives us a far clearer vision of the nature of the problem and the range of potential solutions.

Try Another Approach

My friend's advice didn't really prepare me for my reading (***Railroad Wrecks* by Haine**) on the Mansi railroad accident. It was a horrific event. The deaths of 500 passengers occurred when an overcrowded Indian train stopped suddenly to avoid a cow on the tracks. I would have had a far different perspective on this risk had my friend advised, "They pack people into every nook and cranny of every train over there. And if there's even a minor accident, it will become major." This accident did as the train jumped the rails.

For each of those three events, the risk strategies, the

understanding, and the clarity grow exponentially when the true nature of the event is defined. Even settling on probability and impact becomes a quicker, easier process.

For us, what's the lesson learned? Define the risks clearly and thoroughly. Make them unambiguous enough that they truly add value and understanding. Without that level of clarity, the ability to manage is lost.

* * *

Where Did the Numbers Go?

Living with Risk in a Qualitative Rather Than a Quantitative Perspective

(May 2000)

There's a major push afoot within risk management circles to drive numbers out of risk management. Qualification is being touted as the newfound manna to feed the hungry tribes seeking risk information. Even the Project Management Institute is bending in that direction in the exposure draft to the latest (Y2K) *A Guide to the Project Management Body of Knowledge.* That document layers in a whole new practice of risk qualification as *risk assessment.*

But why? When did numbers take on such a negative taint that they are no longer valued or are perceived as unwieldy or unworthy of our consideration? Just as the computer tools are gaining sufficient speed (and expertise) to actually manage some of the data we can churn into them, as a practice, project managers are backing away from the numerical values. The reason is rooted in something far more significant than levels of effort and statistical accuracy. As a rule, I believe project managers are becoming more honest about the profession.

Numbers are the meat and potatoes of much of project

management practice. The project management software churns out a sea of numbers, without questioning their sources, their roots, their accuracy. One number may come from a veteran with thirty years' experience. Another number comes from a database of historic project information. The third comes from the optimistic rookie without a scar on her back. Yet they are all (in most environments) treated alike. The numbers become the gospel. They become the drivers of the project, their authority unquestioned.

For years, risk practice has enabled this fiction, layering numbers on numbers and multiplying values against values. Finally, the risk community is stepping forward in honesty, saying qualification counts. Qualification, rather than quantification, acknowledges that we cannot see the future, but we can make intelligent guesses about its potential outcomes. Qualification acknowledges differences of opinion on how dangerous or how potentially expensive a particular risk may be. Qualification takes all the annoyances of daily life—politics, personalities, frustrations, past experience—and weaves them into risk consideration through *consistent practice.*

Those last two words are critical. Consistent practice. Organizations seeking the opportunity to implement risk practice consistently will do their best when they clarify the ranges of risk impact and risk probability in consistent terms. When they clarify what constitutes a high-impact risk and what constitutes their threshold of pain as an organization, they have made major strides forward. After that is accomplished, the stage for qualification is set. And the latitude that project managers have taken by ascribing hard values to fuzzy issues begins to wash away.

It's a bandwagon more organizations are jumping on. The first steps are simple. Establish the terms that say this is a high probability. Different people have different perceptions of high probabilities. Clarify what it means. Does it mean distinct possibility or virtual certainty? Ascribe terms and values to ensure that every team member and every project manager consistently applies them. Over time, they become part of the culture. Over time, risk management becomes less of a mystical practice and more integrated.

Should qualification ultimately replace quantification? I don't believe so. When the numbers are available, they should be used. But, in many instances, the numbers are forced. They are works of fiction. And the time for fiction in project risk management is nearing an end.

* * *

Setting the Thresholds

Identifying What the Organization Can and Cannot Handle

(June 2000)

In establishing project plans (and more specifically, risk plans), project managers need to recognize the importance of elements that go beyond basic risk identification and assessment. One critical issue we often miss out on is the notion of the risk threshold. How much can we stand? How much of a schedule delay is too much? How much of a cost overrun can the organization tolerate? The formal, pat answer is often no overruns are acceptable. But that's not realistic. Most projects can withstand some small overruns in terms of schedule or cost, or some small shortcomings in terms of requirements. Those represent our thresholds.

Projects need risk thresholds. Normally, however, they remain unspoken. They're unspoken out of a fear of sharing information that others might take advantage of. They're unspoken because some people dread the notion that they might find themselves in a position where they exceed those limits. Fear should not be a driving force in the reasoning behind risk practice. Risk practice is, by its very nature, a study of those things of which we are fearful. Thus what we need to do is to face those fears and establish, communicate, and promote those thresholds.

We need to share them so that we know what is acceptable in terms of impact. What constitutes a high impact? What constitutes a moderate impact? Without the thresholds, we cannot intelligently answer those fundamental questions. And without the answers to those questions, we cannot effectively prioritize project risk.

The process by which we accomplish this is simple. For cost and schedule, we identify how far is too far. It can be done by asking how many days are tolerable and how much in overruns is tolerable. For requirements, we need to ask where we can afford to give ground and where we can't. In addition to these fundamental thresholds, we should also set the thresholds for politics. How much escalation can the project withstand? How far up the chain of command can complaints or concerns go without creating too much grief? How many calls from the customer are too many? If we establish the answers to these questions at the outset of the project, we clarify the level of risk impact. And we enable the risk process.

Setting tolerances and thresholds starts at the project level. Project by project, we establish these thresholds. As we build a database of understanding on where these thresholds are at the project level, we can begin to identify organizational risk tolerances. Although that's a longer-term effort, it's a critical step toward overall project management maturity. In the ideal, the project office will help project managers establish where they should begin to look at those thresholds and when individual project tolerances exceed organizational tolerance. That's important information because the project has to function in the greater organizational context.

But first, we start small. We start with the incremental step of setting risk tolerance at the project level and generate documentation and history. That documentation should capture the tolerances, how close the project came to the tolerances, and the relative impact of any risks that affected the tolerances. Such information will build the organization's capability to assess risk and, in the long term, manage risk.

* * *

New Risk Practice? Did We Miss Something Before?

Examining the Implications of Change in Project Standards on How We Manage and Mitigate Risk

(September 2000)

A Guide to the Project Management Body of Knowledge (PMBOK® Guide) (Project Management Institute 2008). Zzzzzzzz. I just lost a few of you. It doesn't tend to be dramatic, high-intensity reading. It's the Sleep-Eze of project management. But, it's also setting the standards for what we do. As such, we need to look at how we need to examine our practices in its light.

The Project Management Institute (PMI) issued a major update of the American National Standards Institute (ANSI) Standard of project management, *A Guide to the Project Management Body of Knowledge.* It is now (as of 2009) in its fourth edition. It's a major update and reinforces a lot of great risk content. In fact, during the authorship process, risk management had the distinction of receiving more comments than any of the other knowledge areas did. Does this mean that we've been missing something as practicing risk managers? Had we overlooked some critical issues?

The reassuring words are not really. In fact, the updated *PMBOK® Guide* approach to risk reinforces an enhancement of the practices that effective risk managers should already have had in place. Rather than supplant the old approaches with completely new content, the update simply reinforces some key components of best practice that were implicit in the older version of the *PMBOK® Guide*. The *PMBOK® Guide* looks at what we should have been doing all along.

Specifically, it calls for a consistent risk practice. The risk management plan section acknowledges that too frequently risk is an ad hoc sort of thing. It's not something we manage exactly as our peers do. But with risk management plans, we can begin to build the infrastructure necessary to make it part of our embedded, consistent practices, much like scheduling and budgeting. We can establish consistent thresholds, consistent processes, and consistent interpretations of the data. That's the component of the current *PMBOK® Guide* we'll look at today.

As I drove my son to school the other day, he turned apoplectic as we approached the school's driveway. "Oh no!," he shouted. His eyes darted left and right. "We have to go home." I turned, fully expecting to see blood spurting from a major artery. The urgency of his tone and the panic of the moment led me to assess the risk as high probability/high impact. Pulling over and calming him, I inquired as to the cause of his distress. "I left my trumpet book on the counter. If I don't have it, I'll have to share or borrow one from Mr. Player!"

What's wrong with this picture? Despite my explanation that it was not the end of life as we know it, he remained in despair. We had different standards as to what was worth worrying about and what wasn't. Because we had no standard for "this is what's worth screaming about in Dad's ear and this is what isn't," he took liberties and set the standard as he saw appropriate. His threshold of pain was, by his father's standards, set far too low.

Too frequently, organizationally, we don't know the thresholds of pain. We don't know when management will consider a problem too big to manage or what it would actually take to shut a project down (although many organizations are challenged by that notion altogether). And without that information, one of two conditions may arise. The first is what I now think of as the "trumpet-book syndrome." An innocuous, nonthreatening issue is elevated to unreasonable levels by virtue of the understanding and personal urgency experienced by a given team member. The other extreme is that team members don't know when it's time to escalate. They don't recognize that they have passed into dangerous territory and that they're putting the organization at risk.

For some organizations, a 10-percent variance in cost is normal. For others, it would be catastrophic. In some recent business dealings with two clients, I saw this dichotomy all too well. A start-up Internet enterprise asked for some supplemental work. I quoted a cost of several hundred dollars. The managers balked, hemmed, hawed, discussed, analyzed, and voted before approving it. Another organization I work with asked for a similar level of effort. When I quoted a similar price, the client contact said, "No problem, just add it to your invoice." Note the difference in sensitivity. Note the difference in potential pain. We need to know those thresholds, and we need to set them for more than just cost. Risk thresholds need to be established metrically and organization-wide for the following:

- Cost

- Schedule

- Quality

- Politics

- Customer satisfaction

- And any other issue that can potentially put the organization in peril

If the values can't be set as dollars, days, or percentages, then identify the triggers that indicate we may be in peril (or nearing it). But some clear, unambiguous markers have to be established.

And then they need to be communicated. In the *PMBOK® Guide*, PMI's authors and contributors have gone a long way in identifying the role of the organization in risk management. They have also acknowledged the need for consistency and continuity. We've known it all along. Now, it's just time to apply it.

* * *

A New Take on Risk Management: Project Life in the Aftermath of 9/11

Reviewing the Then-Fresh Impact of 9/11 on Project Management Risk Behavior

(October 2001)

Organizations are talking risk management now more than ever. But are they talking about the right kind of risk management?

I've already taught three sessions of risk management since the 9/11 catastrophe, and it's been compelling to hear the thoughts of students on their organizations' expectations for risk management. For many, the expectations have changed. Rather than the ongoing convention of risk management's being primarily those elements within the project manager's control, many organizations now expect those invested in serious risk management to be seers. They expect the project manager to have insight on how they would handle catastrophes not unlike those that occurred September 11 and those predicted in the days of the aftermath. How unfortunate that it takes disaster to move organizations toward a risk strategy. Also unfortunate is that the types of calamity wreaked on September 11 are precisely those not covered by conventional project risk strategy (save, perhaps, for those in the skyscraper construction or airline industries).

In listening to my students, I hear them talking about how management wants disaster recovery plans of extraordinary detail. Management wants system backups to the system backups. Management seeks assurance that the 9/11 event was an anomaly that in its organization could not happen again.

I contend that is not true project risk management. It's disaster planning. It's recovery planning. It's at the heart of many organizational strategies. But it's a project in and of itself. It's not *project* risk management. Project risk management is the identification, qualification, quantification, and response planning for risks inherent in the project itself. Those external unforeseeable risks that may occur are the stuff of management reserve and disaster recovery plans, not the project risk management plan.

After events like those in September 2001, we're forced to ask if a risk plan won't deal with events of this magnitude, what good is it? Think about the reactions of the people and organizations in the wake of the tragedy. The levels of camaraderie and mutual understanding were remarkable. At airports, people stood in line for hours with extraordinary patience and tolerance. At Fort Detrick, Maryland, the normal "gate wait" of thirty seconds turned into a snaking line of cars that stretched for blocks and hours. Were fingers of blame and accusation turned on project managers whose resources were caught in these snarls? Rarely. Instead, people understood. They empathized. They accepted the delays as being a component of the nature of the catastrophe. It's the nature of management reserve. It's outside the control of the project manager. If anyone wants special dispensation for these extraordinary external events, he needs to go to senior management.

Does this mean that we shouldn't learn from (and in some ways leverage) the events of September 2001? Absolutely not. We learn a great deal from these events. We can draw best from those newly developed strategies. We can build on those miraculous recovery efforts of the days that followed. And we can encourage management to acknowledge where the line should be drawn between project risk management and disaster planning.

For the remainder of this discussion, I'd like to look at what we can leverage from the 9/11 event and how it can integrate into the day-to-day experience of high-quality project management.

Risk Identification: New Perspectives

When it comes to risk identification, the most radical shift that comes from the 9/11 event is a new willingness to talk openly about the possibilities. Anyone who carried on a discussion during the week after the attacks will recall vivid theories about other avenues and means of assault on the United States' national consciousness. People explored their negative fantasies. They examined the worst cases (often with the preface of "Heaven forbid, but ...").

In project risk identification, we will need to temper our team members' new propensity for exploring the wild and lunatic. But we can benefit from a new willingness to accept that although project issues may surface, they cannot be worse than what the United States, as a nation, has endured in recent months. For some people, this has been the first time they have had public license to share their fears, concerns, and paranoia. We should remind them, in as healthy a fashion as possible, that they should take the opportunity to give voice to their concerns rather than masking them. Since September 11, there have been myriad of armchair quarterbacks who have suggested different ways in which the disaster could have been averted. This is their opportunity to be the seers they sometimes claim to be.

First lesson learned from September 11 for project risk management? Get your fears on the table. Explore the negative fantasies that you may have about the project and its future. Open your eyes to the possibilities. Knowing them is the first step toward controlling those that have the greatest likelihood of occurring and the greatest impact.

Risk Qualification/Quantification in the Wake of 9/11

Hyperbole is normally not in short supply in project teams. Those who historically have been willing to share their risks with the remainder of the organization are, on some occasions, those willing to engage in exaggeration about the potential impact or probability of the events. The probability of winning the PowerBall Lottery, for example, was seen by some groups as a high probability during a recent event when the jackpot exceeded one-quarter billion dollars. They would buy a thousand tickets and then envision their probability of victory dropping from 1 in 80,000,000 to 1 in 80,000. They failed to look at it from the perspective that there are still 79,999,000 ways to lose

But, as with the Challenger disaster (another event permanently etched into the memories of those who lived it), we can at least begin to understand the nature of the probabilities associated with risk events through comparison.

Even in the wake of the recent 9/11 tragedy, the odds of dying in an average lifetime of flying are roughly 4,073 to 1. Compare that with the odds of dying in an automobile during a lifetime of driving, 80 to 1! Those are not comforting statistics. Far many more of us fear a three-hour flight than fear a three-hour drive.

So how will this help us qualify and quantify our risks? All these incongruities afford us a defense for sitting down with the team and establishing just what constitutes a high-probability or a high-impact risk. For many organizations, such an evaluation has been long delayed, using the defense that it is superfluous. Now, with team members struggling to reconcile what they should (and should not) worry about, risk qualification (or quantification, if necessary) becomes essential.

How is it done? Through facilitation. Through common language and common terms. Through a mutual understanding of the relative interpretations of probability and impact. In organizations where this has been done in the past, this effort may be relatively quick and painless. For those for whom this represents a first-time endeavor, establishing these terms is a significant level of effort and may require expert internal consulting assistance.

What about Risk Response Development?

This is perhaps where we can draw the greatest insights from the terrorism of September 11. What happened in the wake of the event? Buildings shut down. Offices closed. Some organizations went almost entirely virtual (only to be hit by the Nimda virus later in the week). As if it were ordinary, people did extraordinary things. Money flowed like water into many of the nation's charitable institutions. Around New York and Washington, teams rebuilt communications flows. Alternative messaging systems were created. Different organizations found new ways to churn out information. Normally highly mobile organizations found localized alternatives for implementation.

The organizations that weathered the storm best were those with the infrastructure to manage it. And by infrastructure, I'm not referring to the physical facilities to manage the disaster, but to those who had information and access to the information in the time of need. The New York City Fire Department lost three of its top personnel to the disaster. Yet they knew exactly what to do and how to do it. Why? Because there were protocols and chains of command.

We need to ask ourselves whether such protocols exist in our projects and whether we have taken the time to communicate those protocols with others. In a recent teaching experience, one student emphasized that he would never share information freely because "information is power." I suggest that this attitude is one that has the potential to cripple an organization in true times of need.

I grant that most of us do not have to deal with any catastrophe of this magnitude in our projects (and in many cases, in our lives). But we do need to be braced to handle the lesser problems. And we can learn that if we have the information sharing in place to know who knows what and where the information can be found, and if we are telling others where and how to use that information effectively, then we are taking the tragic lessons of September 11 and putting them to work in the day to day.

The project risk management lessons of September 11 will not be found in the heroic efforts of those who lost their lives that day. They will instead be found in the efforts of those behind the scenes who kept businesses running, those who kept communication flowing, and those who enabled the rest of us to return, albeit slowly, to a relative sense of normalcy. And although the conventional, day-to-day tasks of project management may seem mundane in any comparison, they pay perhaps the greatest tribute to the American ideal. In continuing to live that ideal, we pay at least some small homage to those whose passing served as an intensely painful reminder of that ideal's vulnerability and value.

* * *

Look Out! It's Quality! And It's Headed Our Way!

Connecting with the Resurgence of Quality Practice as Project Management Practice

(April 2002)

As the economy struggles toward a rebound, some organizations are working to make amends for their activities during the economic dip, but they're approaching it in different ways. Some are hiring back staff they released. Some are using the situation to restructure and redefine their business models. Others are looking at process and practice. They're the quality legions, and they have their eyes on project management.

The most familiar practices associated with quality performance are the ISOs. It's a common misconception that ISO stands for International Standards Organization. It does not. ISO is for the Greek "same." That's what ISO is all about, sameness. It is focused on ensuring that business practices are consistent and that the level of quality produced by an organization one day is precisely the same (if not better) in the days, weeks, and months that follow.

There is a variety of different ISO standards. The most familiar is the 9000 series. There is 9000 (International Organization for Standardization 2005), the general quality standards. ISO 9001 is the standard for quality management systems (QMS) (International Organization for Standardization 2008). ISO 9004 is guidance on how to build the QMS (International Organization for Standardization 2000). Many organizations, particularly manufacturing or delivery organizations, are familiar with these ISOs. But there are others. ISO 10005 talks about quality planning (International Organization for Standardization 2005). ISO 10007 is a guideline for configuration management systems (International Organization for Standardization 2003). (Starting to sound a little closer to the project management home?) And ISO 10006 is the guideline (not standard, but *guideline*) for project management (International Organization for Standardization 2003).

Just as this book was being crafted in 2009, the latest edition of *A Guide to the Project Management Body of Knowledge* was released. Just as ISO 9000 and 9001 were updated earlier this decade, 10006 is getting a bit of an overhaul. And with that overhaul comes increased attention. At a time when organizations are looking to improve process and enhance their business posture, the renewed emphasis on 10006 has the potential to bring it out of the shadows and into the project management cultural limelight.

Interestingly, the last time the project management guidelines were updated was in 2003, shortly before the last draft of *A Guide to the Project Management Body of Knowledge.* ISO 10006 has not met with universal accolades; articles have appeared in the project management press deriding the ISO as insufficient guidance to manage a project. The key, however, is that project management is not the focus of the ISO. Quality management in projects is what it's supposed to address, and it does that quite handsomely.

Both the old and the new versions of 10006 simply call out the basic practices, processes, and responsibilities essential to implementing project management well. As project managers, we are afforded a rare opportunity. If we haven't been able to

sell project management internally based on the *PMBOK®
Guide* (Project Management Institute 2008) or on its own
merits, this affords us one more opportunity to drive home
the importance of project management done well.

So there's one more version of project management reality
out there. Is that a bad thing? No, but it's going to be important
to have some measure of control over project management
practice and to build in a level of consistency. Although that's
exactly what project managers have been preaching for the
past fifty years, the difference may come in who's mandating
it. The ISO practices and quality conformance tend to be
the province of a specialized group in many organizations.
Although it's good to have allies, it's important that they
understand the groundwork that's been established. They
should be enlisted as allies, and not perceived (or allowed to
act) as process usurpers.

To ensure this, we project managers need to be proactive.
For many organizations that are ISO adherent, 10006 is a
distant prospect. It is not something that is even on the
radar screen, let alone manifested in organizational process,
procedure, and practice. We need to be the first to take action
to advise our organizations of its existence and the progress
we've already made toward compliance with the guideline.
Again, it is important to emphasize the role of 10006 as a
guideline rather than a standard, as it is not required (but is
desirable) for ISO 9000 certification.

For those organizations already invested in the *PMBOK
®Guide* and the Project Management Institute's processes and
practices, this is not a problem. The ISO guidance and the
PMBOK® Guide have only a few minor points of divergence,
and most of them are manifested in differences in terminology,
not in practice. This means we can continue to apply those
practices we've been applying, but we need to map them into
the various and sundry processes identified in 10006.

What are some of those processes? The existing (2003)

version of 10006 defines strategy, scope, time, cost, communications, risk, purchasing, resources, personnel, and quality processes as essential. This compares to the nine areas of the *PMBOK® Guide,* which calls out integration, scope, time, cost, quality, human resources, communications, risk, and procurement. There's quite a bit of overlap we can exploit to our organization's advantage.

In cost management, for example, ISO 10006 encourages consistent processes for estimating, budgeting, and control. The *PMBOK® Guide* breaks it out as resource planning, estimating, budgeting, and control. There's sufficient overlap to warrant an analysis of compliance with both approaches rather than exclusivity with one.

The beauty of that level of consistency is that it bolsters the argument that project management is not a singular perspective. It doesn't reflect just one person's or group's attitude about how project management is supposed to be done and the practices we're supposed to be following in conducting it. It is the view of managers who have studied management practice globally and who understand what constitutes a successful (and high-quality) project and product deliverable environment.

So what do you need to do first? The first step is to get your hands on a copy of the guideline. One Web reference is the American Society for Quality. The ISO documentation doesn't come cheap, but a single copy of this relatively thin document is well worth the investment.

By knowing what's on the quality horizon, you can begin to predict what's also on the project management horizon, and, as such, you have the ability to build a new set of alliances within your organization. With this insight, you are now capable of defending project management on two fronts rather than just one, with both the Project Management Institute and the International Organization for Standardization behind you. But to build that defense takes knowledge. And it's knowledge that you, as a project manager, need to have in hand now.

Note: ISO's technical committees are currently working on a distinct project management ISO. To date (mid-2009), no significant output has been published.

* * *

Baseline? I'll Do That Later

Establishing the Practices for When It's Time to Set the Baseline

(August 2002)

In my consulting practice and my classroom teachings, I'm finding a common theme regarding the power of (and lack of insight regarding) the simple project baseline. Where do we start? What constitutes underway?

By way of definition, the *baseline* is "the agreed-upon version of the project plan, including the timing, cost, resources, and scope." It's the snapshot of the project against which evaluations are conducted and reviews are built. It's a snapshot that's extremely difficult to take.

Why We Avoid Setting Baselines

In Microsoft Project, the first time a project file is saved, a fateful box invariably appears: *Do you want to save with a baseline?* For many project managers, that's the single most vexing question the tool ever puts to them. If they say yes, are they locking themselves into a project lifetime of misery and woe? If they say no, will the project slowly spiral out of control without warning? Most opt for the no answer, assuming that they'll come back and add data later or come back and finalize the project plan at some future date.

We avoid setting baselines because there are always more data to be had. Management approvals, customer signatures, and team agreements all have the potential to amend the project plan, which (if the baseline were saved) means variance. The yearning for all the data, coupled with a fear of variance, often inspires a near-phobic perspective regarding the baseline. The fear of being tied down to a single set of numbers in some organizations is too much to bear.

In a recent project planning class, I asked a student if he had baselined his network. "No!" he replied defensively, "I'm not ready."

"When will you be ready?" I asked, expecting an answer in terms of classroom minutes remaining. Instead, I got a somewhat philosophical reply.

"We don't have signature from the client on the latest change order, and there's still some dissension on whether we'll get third-quarter funding. Should I have a baseline already?"

Although the classroom answer was yes, I began to ponder the deeper issues this raised. And having had several weeks to think it over, I believe the real-world answer was yes as well.

When to Save the Baseline

It's time to save the baseline when we have agreement. Although no project ever achieves total agreement, the key here is consistency. Pick a document, a signature, an approval, anything. But select some project landmark that is consistent from project to project within the organization. And use it. Make it the marker. Make it the line in the sand that tells us when we're on target and when we're off. And use the same marker for all your projects and, if you're in the project office, all the organization's projects.

Once you select that marker, establish that you will tolerate variance. It doesn't have to be consistent from project to project, but there has to be some tolerance for variance.

If the baseline is set early, that tolerance level must naturally be higher than if the baseline is set only after the work breakdown structure (WBS) is built in excruciating detail from end to end.

If we're going to have variance and we know it can be different from project to project, why bother with a baseline? We need to have a metric by which we can determine whether there are significant deviations. We need to have a tool we can use to identify to the customer what is inside and outside the existing project scope. We need to have the ability to discern whether the project is out of control (or more positively, whether it's complete).

How to Sell Baseline Practice

Why should management or a customer commit to a baseline? Other project managers within the organization may not be as rigid about it, and other contractors may not force the customer to sign off at all. That sometimes makes the job of identifying why we should do best practice more challenging. The rationale for the baseline is that it's in the customer's best interest and provides the customer a defense from the project team.

Most project teams have at least one team member (sometimes the project manager) with vision. You know the person I'm talking about: the individual who sees a project as a learning opportunity with new strategies and tactics to be deployed and new technologies to sample. Vision is not a bad thing if it's tempered by the customer's wishes and aligned with the project plan. But vision can drive a project out of control. And it can do it without anyone's being aware of it, unless there's a baseline. As new tasks are added to facilitate the new vision, a baselined plan should set off alarm bells that there's new work without the authorization to justify it.

As for management or customer vision, the baseline

facilitates that through a controlled, documented change process.

Baselines versus Change

The toughest thing for many organizations to reconcile when setting a baseline is establishing how they'll cope with change. Should they change the baseline? Should they adopt a new baseline? Should the contractor be expected to "eat" the additional expense and squeeze it out of the original baseline?

In preparing for the old Project Management Professional's exam, administered by the Project Management Institute in the early 1990s, there was a question regarding what to do about change in the cost-plus (or cost-reimbursement) contract environment in terms of the baseline. The answer at that time (and I don't know whether it holds true today, but it should) was that major change should be rolled into the project on a firm fixed price (FFP) basis. It should not become part of the new baseline, and it should not become an administrative tracking nightmare as we try to track the original baseline and Baseline II, the Sequel.

Granted, the project planning software will track up to nine different baselines, but that's not terribly helpful when you're trying to apply metrics to determine whether we're ahead of or behind schedule, or over or under cost. That old practice of using FFP to cope with baseline change in the cost-plus environment eases the headache of project tracking, minimizes the cry for baseline changes, and assures some level of consistency. Also, from a practical perspective, if there's a new contract (even a simple FFP), each time the customer wants a change, it will minimize the frequency of such changes. And when they're in place, we'll be able to track them as their own separate entities.

Save with a Baseline?

The answer is yes. After you establish the official organizational benchmark for setting down the tracking practices, and after you clarify how you will handle major change, the yes answer to Microsoft Project's question should be rote. And the more you can consistently set down baselines as an organizational practice, the more you can assure customers (internal and external) that they'll get fair warning when you're straying from the baseline and a clear understanding of what they're getting for what they're investing.

* * *

Measure Me!

Assessing How We Can Set Metrics the Team
Can Live with and That Reflect What the Organization
Really Needs to Know

(February 2003)

The scale is my enemy. Really. I hate it. As I step on and watch the dial whirl under the needle, I pray for a number I can live with. I never get that number. So I'll take a break from it and come back in a few months. Maybe it will have softened by then. Or maybe I'll get my cholesterol number. Or my body fat percentage. Odds are I won't like any of the numbers, but who knows? There may just be one out there that makes me feel better about all of it.

I've just finished a one-day workshop with a group of project professionals on project metrics. We skipped past the conventional metrics of earned value and milestone variance into the more esoteric territory of portfolio metrics and risk metrics. After it was over, one participant asked if there weren't more. Maybe he wanted his cholesterol number.

Metrics are compelling things. They have the allure of being a potential panacea for project ills. They will identify which projects to work on first, which projects deserve the most resources, which projects are the highest risks, and which projects serve the organization best. But it depends on which metrics you apply. A portfolio model may indicate the project meets a host of strategic objectives but may not identify the relative risk. A risk model may identify the relative risk but not the resource consumption. A ratio of resource use to profit may show effective utilization in terms of current dollars but may erode the organization's infrastructure.

In fact, that student's request for more metrics was probably well grounded. But it's not just more metrics we need. We need the right metrics. We need to find the metrics that accurately reflect the culture, the organization and its capabilities, and how projects fit into that mix. Invariably some customization seems to be required. But that creates its own set of headaches. If we customize metrics, we may lose the ability to evaluate our organizations in the context of other organizations that apply the same metrics. We may also delude ourselves into believing we're better than we are.

(As an aside, I had a scale once that consistently made everyone over 200 pounds 15 pounds lighter. I dearly miss that scale.)

Which Metrics Are Right?

The right metrics are those that accurately afford a consistent understanding of where projects and organizations stand at a given time versus how they stood at another time. They reflect what matters most to the organization and how those within the organization are judged. The are both reflective and predictive, looking to the past and the future.

The right metrics are also those that have some proven

validity over time. Earned value is popular, in part, simply because it has been around for such a long time. There is a relative sense of how bad a 0.62 cost performance index (CPI) might be and an understanding of the uselessness of schedule performance index (SPI) at the end of the project (where it eventually, always, hits 1.0).

If we're going to use new metrics or organizationally specific metrics, we will have to give them time to prove themselves. Without the time to evaluate whether the metrics actually serve our long-term interests, their information is as valuable as stepping on a neighbor's bathroom scale. Yes, some information is provided, but its real meaning may be obscured because we don't know or understand what it means.

The other issue that should be considered in determining whether the right metric is being applied is whether it answers the question we're asking. Weight on a scale doesn't report on body fat. Earned value doesn't reflect team satisfaction. Customer satisfaction metrics don't reflect on corporate sustainability. Selecting the right metric means looking at project after project after project and asking which measurement really lets us know that x is happening or will happen?

It may be organizationally dependent. In some organizations, customer satisfaction is clearly tied to customer retention. In others, earned value and CPI numbers may directly reflect the probability of technical success. But this won't be the case in all organizations.

How Do We Know?

Perhaps the most effective way to establish the right metrics is to reverse engineer the entire process. By examining past projects and weighing them as they would be weighed under new metrics, we can get a relative sense of the potential for success with the metrics. For example, if seven projects that were highly technically successful all had CPIs of 93 percent or higher, we may have discovered a valid metric. If that same sample is tainted by four abysmal failures that had CPIs of more than 93 percent, it may indicate that the earned value metric is not appropriate in this particular instance.

In the rush to measure, some organizations are pushing hard to assign and establish meaning for numbers. In reality, those numbers may be meaningless. By working back from older projects and finding out what made them tick, we may be able to discern which metrics are the true arbiters of success.

Do We Want to Know?

The other key question that must be asked for any organization is do we really want to know the numbers the system or process may generate? When I step on the scale, I know then that I really didn't want to know because I'm not prepared to act on the information. If your organization begins the slow crawl toward accurate metric measurement, it's completely fair to push back and ask how the numbers will be used, how they will affect behavior and performance, and whether they'll be around for the long term. If we're simply marking time until a better metric is developed, we might be wiser to save organizational time and energy by waiting until we have a metric we can truly use.

And if we do want to know and have found meaningful metrics, success will largely be rooted, in the long term, by how long we use the same measure. Time is one of the great validators of metrics.

* * *

The Mail Must Go Through

What the Postal Service, Fed Ex, UPS, and DHL Can Teach Us about Better Ballpark Estimates

(September 2004)

I received a package this week that I had purchased on eBay. Nothing exciting. Just a 1950s ice crusher for my somewhat retro kitchen. As I unwrapped my prize, I began to consider how amazing it was that it had made the journey safely from its owner to me. I also considered how it was truly a project to get it from point A to point B. There was a specific objective, an approach, a unique set of environmental circumstances, and a (perceived) limit on time. The project models apply well, but the delivery organizations have their own considerations that might teach project managers a thing or two.

Consider the delivery model for any of the major carriers. They have a relatively consistent set of metrics that project managers might be prudent to consider. Specifically, when it comes to building the ultimate in parametric cost models, each carrier has one set of metrics that is consistently applied: size, weight, and distance. Those three dimensions can actually help us as project managers as we strive to establish ballpark estimates for our organization—if we can morph them into our cultures.

Size

How does this fit with other work that the organization normally does? What range of costs is associated with projects of that scale? If the project is enormous, ask what percentage of the organization's total effort will be expended on the project in the year ahead. In small organizations, a major project may consume as much as a fourth of its total level of effort. As such, consider the annual expenses of the company as the model for a starting point on cost. If the organization is a billion-dollar enterprise, then an effort that takes as much as a tenth of the resource pool better be at least a $100 million proposition. If the organization does $250,000 annually, then an effort that consumes a month of the organization's time starts in the $20,000–30,000 range.

Weight

Sometimes, even large projects will carry themselves on their own momentum. Others need to be pushed. Hard. The more intervention and oversight a project requires, the more it will cost. Consider a percentage premium for each time management has to touch the project in a given month. Think about the organizational capital that's involved. Lighter projects don't require much senior-level intervention. They can be handled by middle management or individuals at the task level. But some projects involve bigger clients or clients who believe they merit special attention. For those efforts, you have to put on weight. You have to bring in "heavier" personnel: vice presidents, supervisors, managers. If you have a general idea of how much the project should cost, start increasing that value every time you envision it putting on weight.

Distance

How far does this project reach? The reach of a painted room is limited. The reach of a new production line is significant. Distance relates to how long the project will be expected to last and how many different corners of the organization might be involved. All too often, ballpark estimates fall short because we consider only the deliverable, not the distance that has to be covered to deliver it. If we can learn from the carriers, we'll recognize that, particularly for the projects of significant size and weight, there's a premium on distance as well.

The Point

When it comes to establishing our own personal cost models, think very carefully about how the major carriers do it. If it's small, compact normal business (a #10 envelope or a standard Express Letter), we should have some standard fees in mind. Weight and distance won't be issues. We know what we're capable of and what it costs. Be we should be wary of those clients who try to "overstuff that envelope." As they increase the weight or the distance, we need to take pause and review whether they've stepped over the line. Federal Express has an interesting note on its envelope: "If the gross weight of the contents, FedEx Envelope, and air bill exceeds eight ounces, the next higher rate will apply." For customers who try to nudge us into "lighter" estimates, the more we can do to standardize like our peers in the delivery industries, the more ready we'll be to serve with a better and more honest and accurate estimate.

* * *

Unraveling the Mystery of the Milestone

*How the Milestone Keeps Us and Our Teams
Moving Forward*

(September 2008)

As I write this article, I'm on final approach into Las Vegas, Nevada. The pilot on this particular flight has served as both driver and tour guide, pausing at four intervals along the way to greet the passengers and to highlight local sites of interest 30,000 feet below.

"The city down to the right of our flight is St. Louis, Missouri, Gateway to the West."

"If you look out the left side of the aircraft, that's Lake Powell."

What's notable is his effective use of milestones. It's been textbook, which makes you wonder whether it's by design or happenstance. In our projects, it definitely should be by design, and we should seriously consider the implications of the decisions we make in that regard.

What Makes a Good Milestone

A good milestone meets specific criteria:

- It acknowledges significant accomplishment.

- It can be defined as "done" or "not achieved" without a great deal of investigation.

- It occurs after some time has passed since the last milestone.

- It's something that those involved may actually care about.

The Pennsylvania Turnpike is a long, challenging stretch of road. And the folks responsible for the turnpike used to have a clear understanding of the nature of milestones. They accomplished the effective application of milestones using rest stops and service areas. Spaced a little more than an hour apart, these highway oases provided a lovely break from the drive and a sense that genuine progress toward the long-distance driving goal was being achieved. Fast forward to the 1990s and 2000s, however, and you'll find a number of changes along that highway that have changed the sense of efficacy the road used to have. First, they've closed a number of the rest areas. It's now possible to drive for more than two hours without encountering a single structured break.

And secondly, they've added minimarkers—small posts with numbers that identify each tenth of a mile traveled—between the conventional mile markers.

Significant Accomplishment

A tenth of a mile. That's not very long. At sixty-five miles per hour, it takes less than six seconds to cover that distance. 142.5 … 142.4 … 142.3 …. Driving several hundred miles, that's quite a bit of counting. I'm certain those mile markers were not meant simply to be milestones for the weary traveler, but they do serve that function. They provide the ability to track just how much distance has been covered and how much farther there is to go. But they grow wearisome. In fact, although the intent may be to clearly identify location and progress to date, for the exhausted wayfarer, they can suck the life out of you. The reason is that nothing significant has been accomplished. No real ground has been covered.

This applies in project life as well. We need to avoid giving team members such minute incremental progress reports that they don't get a sense that they're ever going to accomplish anything dramatic. When life is a series of tiny nonevents, there's the distinct possibility that you're going to lose sight of the big things that really do matter.

By contrast, the rest areas used to have a reasonable span from one to the next. And, oddly enough, that mattered. Knowing that you were coming up on those buildings with their stone faces gave you a sense that you had arrived, even though you were still hours from your destination. The sense of arrival came because there was an emotional attachment and significance to the locations. Even if you didn't stop, you found comfort on the road, knowing that you had achieved something significant.

The lessons here are legion. Create a milestone with an emotional tie, and you win. Create a milestone that allows for reasonable breaks, and you win. Create milestones that capture the essence of significance, and you win. Create something recognizable and clear, and you win.

The compelling part about this is that it doesn't require a deeply held set of beliefs to work well. It just requires an understanding that human beings develop an emotional attachment when they learn to know what to expect from a situation. We develop attachments when we believe that others have similar attachments. Milestones can develop significance if we empower them by finding ways to endow them with these characteristics. In some cases, that involves little more than identifying them and letting others know what they mean. In other cases, sheer repetition is the key.

No matter the approach, we need to work toward and consider the next milestone. It's one of those things where we can make a concrete step today. This is a wondrous opportunity to improve our lives and our projects with a single, small step forward. One new milestone can give us new targets to shoot for and new perspectives on progress.

* * *

Process: Executing

Touching the Customer in the Moment of Truth

*Examining the Implications of the "Baby Steps" of
Any Project and How They May Influence
Our Customer Relationships*

(October 2000)

There's a concept in quality circles that bears serious consideration and investigation in project management. It's a concept originally developed by the Scandinavian airline SAS and now pursued by many organizations that take quality seriously. It's called "moments of truth" (MoT). Moments of truth are the key moments of customer contact. The late Ron Zemke, a well-known author of quality topics, posits that moments of truth occur any time we have the chance to make a significant impression on the customer (Zemke 1990).

In the project context, this occurs frequently—sometimes more frequently than we care to consider. We touch the customer when the customer works with our team members. We touch the customer when we reveal our internal operations. We touch the customer any time our personnel or our products/services generate an emotion.

I recently purchased a new software application and considered this concept in that environment. My first MoT came when I spotted an advertisement in an in-flight magazine. It was a positive moment. The ad made an impression. I tore the advertisement out of the magazine. The manufacturer won the first (albeit small) battle. The next MoT came when I ordered online. Another win! The transaction was smooth, and the interface provided an aura of tight security as I input my credit card information. To date, I was a happy customer. When a week passed without the software's arrival, another MoT occurred. It was my first call to the service line. This time, a confusing "Push-4-if-you-want-to-talk-to-Bob" routing system degraded my impression of the manufacturer's performance. I eventually found the right human being, but the esteem of the organization dropped. The next MoT? The manufacturer delivered the software. Nice package, easy loading and registration. Good work. The next? A call to technical support to clear up a glitch. And so on.

By the time I had the software up and running for the first time, the company had already had half a dozen opportunities to make or break their relationship with me as a customer. How does this tie in to project management? It ties in in two places. The first is customer management. If we are not considering our MoTs, then we are not looking at how the relationship is going to evolve. The second is in my corner of the project universe—risk management.

This may seem an unlikely topic for a discussion on risk management, but it's not. I firmly believe that if we invest the time to investigate our MoTs, we open the door for a clear understanding of where we are at the greatest risk. Think of a relay race. The great risk? The handoff. Coaches study the handoff fastidiously. They analyze and critique it. MoTs are handoffs of our image to others. And if we fail to give them the attention they merit, we risk exposure of our greatest organizational problems.

I recently called a client and asked to speak to a particular team member. The receptionist said, "I don't think anyone works here by that name." I knew he did and eventually convinced the receptionist to review the employee phone list. For my client, that would be an MoT. Were I a customer, rather than a vendor, I would have suddenly developed serious doubts about the organization's administrative capabilities. I would have been worried that it would loses files. I might have been concerned that it rotates staff so quickly that no one knows who really works there. The impressions could be devastating.

But what can we, as project managers, do about resolving these MoTs? We can identify them in advance. Planning through and planning for the MoTs gives us a corporate edge. It encourages the levels of proactivity that make us good at our craft. It's also a simple way to communicate to the organization what concerns we have about its interactions in our projects. By predicting when and how the MoTs will occur, we afford our organizations one more avenue for understanding the myriad interactions involved in every project. By communicating our expectations for the MoTs, we mitigate risk.

* * *

Victims of Success: How Do We Communicate up in a Culture of Success?

Parsing Through Our Relationships with Upper Management for Communications Success

(January 2001)

Reporting risk is easy. It's a matter of sharing information through classical means. But in today's cultures of success, the problem is frequently associated with the challenge of getting management to accept negative news when the outcomes belie the information being provided. How do we give bad news when management isn't accustomed to hearing it?

This discussion was actually rooted in a recent class. A student raised the question, forcing me to think it through and to consider the alternatives and options. Today's dot-com wonders point to precisely the environment the student envisioned. Dot-coms are classic for their shortsighted realities, dripping in success, when they should be considering the potential for negative long-term consequences. NASA encountered this in the Challenger disaster, and the experience was thoroughly documented in Diane Vaughan's tome, *The Challenger Launch Decision* (Vaughan 1997). Vaughan analyzes the accident in depth and invests most of her discussion in the issues generated by a culture of success at NASA. She points to the rapid-fire series of successes in the face of potential disaster (including the STS mission just before Challenger) and NASA's growing sense of invulnerability at the time.

In a seminar recently with one of my clients, we discussed the same issue in a commercial environment. The organization had a gift for selecting projects well and for culling out the projects that didn't merit its efforts. As a result, the organization began to develop an attitude that "failure is not an option." Concurrently, management developed an attitude that risk was the purview of the project manager rather than the organization as a whole. Although those are not inherently problematic perspectives, they may become so because project managers feel they are being discouraged from sharing any potential bad news. As long as the organization continues to pick projects for which it is truly capable and knowledgeable, and able to manage the risks at the project level, project managers will succeed. But if the risk climate in the organization changes (as it may during a merger that's underway) the very culture of risk management will have to change.

In a best-practice environment, they're not taking this lightly. They've begun developing risk checklists and risk models that will elevate visibility on project risks. Some project managers in the organization hold out hope that this will give them greater license to share information about risk with senior management. It may, and if the organization is to continue to flourish in an environment of change, it must. Although they may continue to function in an environment where failure is not an option, they must help team members, managers, marketers, and senior management to be attuned and alert to the very real risks that will evolve in the years to come.

* * *

Don't Have a Job? Consult Your Way to a New One

A Look at How a Consulting Mentality Can Drive Us to Progressively Better Management Behaviors

(March 2002)

Let's examine what happens if you're among the legions who are staring at project unemployment in challenging economic times. Seeking new work is always daunting, and most find it still more challenging when they are unemployed. The solution? Employ yourself.

I jumped willingly into the unemployment pool almost four years ago, declaring myself a free agent from my former (and best) employer, ESI International. After more than eight years in its service as a full-time employee, I determined that the only way I could possibly find a better boss would be to work for myself. Since that time, although the work has had its ups and downs, my annual income has seen significant increases; I've gained greater control of my schedule; and I've actually turned away at least four job offers. But do you have what it takes to consult your way to a new job? Or to consult your way to independence? Consider some of the paths to success:

- Public relations (PR)

- Diversity

- Enthusiasm

- Conformity

- Value

Public Relations

You're unemployed. You just became your own public relations agency. You are now responsible for making your name a household word—somewhere. How do you do that? The biggest question you have to answer is what do I do well that others struggle with? It's a tough question. Humility historically precludes us from touting our own capabilities. This is no time to be humble. The Project Management Institute (PMI) has meetings—use them! Volunteer as the speaker. One of the greatest nonpaying speaking engagements I ever had was teaching project management to ... get ready ... a kindergarten class. Did it win me any work? No. Did it help me find new ways to share the project management gospel? Indeed! I've used some of the tricks I've used with six-year-olds to explain PM to corporate executives. You want to spread your name around any way you can. Here are some venues to consider.

- www.projectconnections.com (blatant self-promotional moment): Message boards should be replete with your insights on every PM discussion you can find. This is a fine place to start.

- PMI newsletters: There are dozens of PMI chapters out there, each publishing its own newsletter and often desperate for articles. Poof! You're an author. And you can cite the publication on your resume, and you become the expert in your field of endeavor, and you get visibility.

- Professional meetings: PMI gets its fill. If you're working in the engineering community, offer to speak at the Institute of Electrical and Electronics Engineers. In the media? Consider PM for the American Federation of Television and Radio Artists/Screen Actors Guild. In purchasing or procurement? How about PM for the National Association of Purchasing Management? Put those professional association memberships to work.

You cannot be too present. You need to get out and participate. Church and civic committees, university relationships, and professional associations all have roles in building professional networks. Because you're a PR firm of one, you have no one to blame but yourself if you don't get the word out. Write articles. Coauthor articles with more prominent consultants. Show yourself off.

Diversity

Ask someone from Enron about the value of a diverse portfolio. Ouch! Similarly, you are not going to have your greatest success from a single folder within your portfolio. The more things you can do well, the more effective you'll be as a consultant. The key is to ensure that they are things you can do well and concurrently.

Consider the following list of opportunities available to the project management consulting professional:

- Training

- Managing projects

- Scheduling using the tools (e.g., Microsoft Planner, Primavera, Artemis)

- Keynote speaking

- Ghost writing

- Expert witness

- Team facilitation

- Project reviews

- Tools development

- Article writing

- PM sales

- PM tools sales

- PM training sales

- PM case research

- Project office coaching

- Project office infrastructure development

And this list could go on.

Enthusiasm

You're looking for work. This is not the most gung ho moment of your life. I don't care. Neither do those who are hiring consultants. They want gung ho. They seek zeal. If you don't have it, they can find a consultant who does. This doesn't mean that you're an animated machine. It means you are passionate about your topic, energized by the opportunities it presents for you and their organization, and hopeful about the prospects of how you can improve their PM practice.

To show some zeal for the work and the organization, you have to be equally excited about what you are able to do. The old phrase goes, "There is no *I* in *team*." I contend that *me* is in there though. And that reinforces the notion that you can't be an energizing force on the team if you're not an energizing force for yourself. Fake it for a while if you have to. It will start to come more naturally over time.

Conformity

You've always been different. Me too. Hair to the shoulders. Life in T-shirts. It was great. I used to show up for my postcollegiate jobs in shorts and a T-shirt. I also made $200 a week. If corporate dress is a kilt and pipes, get used to plaid. Sacrifice your individuality? If that's what it takes to be part of their culture, make some changes. You don't have to turn into an Orwellian clone, but you do need to blend in. Make it so that writing a check to you is just as natural as starting the morning coffee. Don't make it a bone of contention for your sponsors in the organization. If they have to defend you, let it be over your performance, not your look.

Value

What are you worth? $200 a day? $400? $3,000? $6,000? Don't undersell yourself. And don't oversell yourself. Know your worth. I have more than half a dozen different job titles. No two pay the same. For work I can do from my basement in my robe and bunny slippers, I charge far less than for a day of consulting on the road. If an opportunity may lead to myriad other pieces of work from a variety of clients, I charge less than if it's a one-time experience. Build in the proposal and development costs. Build in the time you'll invest in creating a relationship. And then put a stake in the ground on what you're worth. It's a good idea to find out what organizations are paying for their employees for fully loaded rates for the same function. You should make that much or more if you serve the same function. If you bring a unique skill set to the table, then you should get paid for the investment of time, energy, and insight through the years. You're worth more for the topics you know well than you are for those where you're doing the learning curve on the sponsor's nickel.

Could you be worth $3,000 a day or more? Is it a short, one-time experience? Is it something for which you have to do extensive legwork and research? Are you one of the best in the world at doing it? Do you have the credentials to prove it? Have you invested extensive time in building the relationship? Are you providing support beyond the onsite engagement? Is extensive travel involved? For each no answer, you can deduct as much as $500 and sometimes more, depending upon your strength in other areas. If you can answer yes to all those questions, you're probably a high-powered consultant who can command that much or more in the right situation.

It's also vital to know what the market will bear. You may be worth $1,000 a day, but if the sponsor is paying others only $200 a day for the same skills, you'll never get your rate. But, you may be able to reshape your relationship. What would it take to make it worth your while to work for $45 an hour? Work at home? On your schedule? On a filler basis when you have the time? Although the $300-an-hour jobs are wonderful, they aren't always there. Finding something that can fill the gaps keeps you sharp and financially balanced at the same time. One day in your robe at $45 an hour is better than a full day with no income.

What's of value right now? It depends. What will you leave behind? If you're just pushing paper for a day, you won't be leaving anything too memorable behind and shouldn't expect a rate like the high-powered consultants from the Big Six consulting firms. If you're leaving a legacy of quality practices, access, and tools, you may be able to outdraw even the big fish in the pond.

You don't get there by playing it close to the vest. Secrecy and a proprietary attitude are not tools a consultant should use. We win by being ready to add value to our sponsoring organization's bottom line. We share, share, share, share, share. Do that, and the rewards will follow. But know what those rewards should be, and then cut your clients a modest break. Suddenly, you're the best show in town.

Where Does It Lead?

The frightening part of all this is that consulting, done well, is addictive. It's entirely possible to find yourself in a situation where you are enjoying working for a variety of organizations so much that you no longer wish to work for a single entity. I joke with my wife, Nancy, that I've been unemployed for four years. It's gainful, exciting, and engaging unemployment that I could have given up a dozen times because of job offers I've had. I never would. I consulted my way to a new job. But instead of having a single employer, I now have dozens, and I respect them deeply, appreciate their commitment to the profession, and am honored to serve them. It's important to remember that your next job might have a completely different look, feel, and approach from the type you're accustomed to. And if you truly love it, poof! You're a consultant.

* * *

I Promise: Some Summertime Thoughts on Promises We Should Make to Ourselves, Our Organizations, and Our Project Teams

Communicating, Empowering, and Team Building in One Fell Swoop

(July 2002)

I am counting down the days to my annual vacation at the beach. Of course, my idea of a vacation may not be like everyone else's. I tend to cut back to doing my e-mail only twice a day and to work only a couple of hours a day on my ongoing projects. To me, that's just about as close to total isolation and quiet time as I can possibly stand.

But in the waning days of my summer busy season, I had the good fortune to hear former New York City Mayor Rudy Giuliani speak on project management (at a project management lovefest in NYC), and his thoughts reverberated on what it takes to run a project and to have an environment in which we're both accountable and feeling rewarded for our projects. In light of his insights and his shared experiences, I felt compelled to make a few promises.

I Promise to Have a Vision and to Let Others Know Where I'm Going

Ready to head on vacation? I don't want to leave my team members wondering what I expect while I'm away. The key is to let others know where we're going to go. We can't assume that they're going to have a clear understanding of what's coming up if we don't tell them. Mayor Giuliani talked about the people he trusts and the reasons he trusts them. And a big part of it is that they share his vision. They understand it. They can communicate it with some of the same fervor he does. That's crucial. As I head for the beach, I want to know that although my toes are sifting through the warmth of the summer sand, the team is going to be addressing concerns and dealing with customers in the same fashion I would.

How will I communicate it? I'll write it down. I'll craft a project vision statement. I'll catalog my objective with clarity. I'll hang it on posters on the wall. It's not something to be left to chance. We need a common understanding.

Don't expect everyone to see what you see. They can't. They don't. And when you're not there, you need to leave a road map to lead the way. That's essential. Part of that is communicating information in a way they can see and understand. Don't feel that you need to embellish it. Just make sure you leave reminders about where you're going on that road map and why.

When you get back from vacation, if you've left the project in good hands and with a clear understanding of where you're headed, you have only one new question to ask: how much closer are we than when we left?

I Promise to Take Advantage of the Authority Granted to Me and to Grant It to Others

One other thought that Rudy shared was the notion that we need to take advantage of the authority we're granted.

Uh, Carl? I wasn't granted any authority.

Oh, but you were. The authority to build the schedule. The authority to deal with the customer. The authority to share information with the team.

No, it doesn't sound like authority until you actually deploy it. If you do deploy it well, you'll find yourself in the position where you're in charge. But no sooner are you in charge than you're going on vacation. What do you do? You build your authority—by giving it away.

Tell others what you can do. Tell others how they can serve. Tell them what they have control over and what they don't. By giving them authority, you ensure a greater chance of project success while you're gone and you build their respect for you (even in your absence) by respecting them and their capabilities.

I Promise to Get Something Done

Progress is everything. I intend to make some at the beach. I intend to forge my way through two *New York Times* Sunday crosswords, one tacky beach novel, and a few articles. Does this advance the profession, my projects, and my team? Yes!

It buys me and my team members a sense of balance. It lets them know that I respect their desires for a reasonable level of rest and relaxation. It also gives them a chance to get something done and prove themselves capable of taking their organizations forward in my absence.

The Promise of Summer

The promise of summer is in the future of our projects and, in many cases, in the future of our projects without us. That doesn't make us lesser project managers. It makes us greater. It makes our team members more. And it gives us a chance to breathe.

Sand castles, anyone?

* * *

Project Management Starts with PR: Branding Project Management

Providing Insight on How We Can Leverage Our Skills into True Public Relations

(October 2003)

Coca-Cola. McDonald's Golden Arches. The two most recognizable brands on the planet. No matter the city, state, or country, you know precisely what to expect. When you think of Coke, do you think of a gourmet quaff? Of course not. It's Coke, for crying out loud! When you think of McDonald's, are you expecting top sirloin, ground to order, just the slightest hint of pink at the center of the ground patty? Don't be silly. And yet, they are major forces in the economy. They are big players one can, one burger at a time.

What's your brand of project management? Does it vary from client to client? If so, you may have a problem. Branding is, if nothing else, a lesson in consistency. When someone decides that you are the right project manager for the job, what kind of PR are you using to sell yourself as consistent? Internally or externally, we have a brand. Some project managers are the "get-out-of-my-way-or-I'll-flatten-you-like-a-grape" project managers. Others are the "how-can-I-help-you-today?" project managers. But some folks think that "situational management" means situational approaches to how we manage our efforts. That's a more people-oriented practice and a subject for a completely different article. Project management and the public relations that make it effective are rooted in effective and consistent practice.

Figuring out Your Brand

What are you known for? When people think of you in your professional life, what do they expect? It's more than just what you're good at. I consider myself a decent writer, but most folks don't perceive me as a writer. It's not part of my brand. Brand is based on the outside looking in. It's focused on how others see you. If you want to change your brand, you don't change the inside nearly as much as you change the perceptions of others assessing you.

When others think of me professionally, they think of my_____. Is it sense of humor? Frenzy? Chaos? Charts? Graphs? To-do lists? Bounce-off-the-walls enthusiasm?

However you finish that sentence is a first step in identifying your existing brand. Queen of the Flip Charts? The Lord of Post-its? Master of the Leatherette Three-Ring Binder? You are known for something. And you have to identify what you're known for before you can identify your brand. All project managers work to deliver projects. How they deliver them is their brand.

Many project managers go through life without a brand. That's because they don't strive to optimize or focus on the one or two things for which they're known. They don't call attention to their brand. That may be in part because brand can be both a blessing and a curse. Ask ValuJet. The airline had a clear recognizable brand name, and the brand screamed "inexpensive." When the Everglades tragedy occurred, the brand became a curse.

In setting down your brand, you need to know what you're known for, and you need to know how you deliver that brand. One project manager I've had the honor of working with is an ESI Executive VP named LeRoy Ward. LeRoy has a clear and distinct brand: credibility. Every interaction, every element of his professional demeanor drips with credibility. He does an executive meeting? He's direct, straightforward, and credible. He stands in front of a slide with Larry, Moe, and Curly? He still finds a way to be credible. He does it by knowing what he's talking about and staying focused and on topic. If someone steers him away, he steers them back. It's his gift. But his brand is more than his professional capability. He looks the part as well. Even on business casual days, he's pressed and neat. And he talks the part. Whether in a casual conversation or a rehearsed presentation, he's focused and can redirect the conversation at will. He's the consummate professional and rarely strays from his brand image. It's inspired.

By contrast, my brand is that of "rumpled risk/project management comic/pundit." I could never pull off LeRoy's brand. And I shouldn't even try. Why? I'm a different brand. He's Coke. I'm Pepsi. That's fine.

When you think about what people expect of you, it comes in a variety of forms. They expect dress, demeanor, behaviors, and habits. Shift from those behaviors and you become New Coke. (For those who don't recall the New Coke debacle, on April 23, 1985, the Coca-Cola Company unveiled a reformulation of the core cola product. By July 1985, they were apologizing and announcing their intention to return Old Coke to the shelves). We want clear expectations and familiarity. We want people to know what to expect. Consider the following aspects of brand from the cola wars:

- Cost

- Appearance

- History

- Product

- Aftertaste

Now think about those elements in your project management practice. Are you the most expensive of your peers or the cheapest? Are you the navy blazer or the cotton khakis? Are you the grizzled veteran or the fresh face? Do you deliver slowly and steadily or in bursts of incredible energy? Do you follow up consistently or simply respond to requests? Each of those components goes to establishing your brand. None is better than the other. They are largely dependent upon your capability and customer taste.

Using Your Brand

An interesting side note to the New Coke episode in the

1980s: Coke conducted taste tests before introducing New Coke. Customers preferred the new taste by a significant margin. What Coke failed to recognize, however, was the incredible power of brand loyalty. They had built a brand that people loved, honored, and cherished. People were not buying just a bottle of taste. They were buying everything about it, including a hundred-year history of performance. They were buying what they knew.

We can take a powerful lesson from this episode only if we know or explore our own brands. By building a brand, people learn to set and accept expectations. Part of my personal brand is the American idiom. I speak American idiomatic English with the best of them. When I went to take on an opportunity in Sweden, I was warned to leave the idiom behind. I didn't. I couldn't. It's part of who I am. And it's part of my brand. And although some of the Americanisms may have left my Swedish peers wondering, the fact that I was acting precisely as they had seen me act in the States built even more brand loyalty and trust. My reception couldn't have been warmer.

We use our brand by doing what we do and sharing it in the same fashion in each project experience.

Does every project manager have to have a brand? No. You can still purchase generic cola at the supermarket. But for many buyers, such a purchase would be heresy. For others, they're perfectly comfortable with whatever flows from the can. But if you want your performance to be a key component of future decisions, brand loyalty will definitely work in your favor.

* * *

What Makes You Listen? Getting Messages Across

Tricks and Tips on More Effective Ways to Communicate

(July 2004)

"From the gunner's seat of an M-1 tank, I'm Carl Pritchard." I used to have a career in the media (proof that project management is the accidental profession). And that is one of the more memorable phrases that I was ever privileged to utter on the air. I was the news guy. And one of the objectives in media is the same as one of the key objectives in project management: get others to listen to you. What is interesting is that the message often isn't as important as the setting. And in many instances, we forget about some of the basics of good, clear, effective communication.

Having now become the risk management guy, I know about the pain associated with communicating messages. Risk is generally perceived as bad news. Justifiably so. It's tough to listen to information about all the bad things that could happen. It's even tougher when the message can just as easily be ignored. One student recently shared that her boss told her, "My projects just don't have risk. Period." This is the professional moral equivalent to jamming fingers into your ears and humming your favorite tune. Getting messages through to people is no mean feat. But there are ways to accomplish it. People cut through the interference all the time. To be consistent about it, the key is to ensure you have the ability to recognize that different elements make messages attractive to different people. Messages can be rendered more attractive through history, setting, and personal influence.

The Stories

We all have our favorite stories. If you're married, you've heard your spouse's favorite stories dozens of times. You may even be able to mimic the inflection and pacing of the tale. They're familiar. And yet, we don't tire of them nearly as readily as we tire of hearing other information because they have a sense of personal influence and depth that is not common in other settings. Stories create common bonds. The story of Moses and Pharaoh. The story of Helen and Paris in Troy. The story of the world-record soccer field. Oh? Never heard the last one?

In July 1994, the Washington DC-area landscaping firm of Ruppert Landscape hosted a one-day competition to motivate its employees. A total of 425 professional landscapers descended on a packed-dirt, hardscrabble, trashy dust bowl to convert it to a lush, green, playable soccer field. Total time elapsed? Twenty minutes. In just twenty minutes, they ripped down vines that had crept up light poles, prepared the soil, carted off the trash, and sodded an entire soccer field. Twenty minutes of antlike activity, crawling across an Adams-Morgan field, coordinated to perfection and moving across the field with drill team precision.

You have a new story. It's even a project management story. It's a story that could be used to talk about the awesome power of teamwork. Or the inspired efforts associated with effective planning. Or it could be used to address the nature of short-cycle-time projects. Stories can be twisted to our needs. But if someone tells you that private-public partnerships are important, that's one thing. Without the story, that statement is weak. Telling you that story, and citing the press coverage that survives an entire decade, is another thing. People will remember the twenty-minute soccer field. And they are more likely to remember the message that goes with the story if they know the story and it's told well.

The Setting

Life presents us with wondrous opportunities, and the cell phone has gone a long way toward sharing those opportunities. Most of us have either called or received a call from some bizarre, exotic locale. Just recently, on Atlanta's MARTA system, I overheard a gentleman saying, "You won't believe this. I'm on the subway in Atlanta. We're underground, and I still have a signal." He was sharing the setting. He was drawing in the person on the other end by trying to get that person to marvel at the experience with him.

I remember recording stories for the news inside an M-1 tank, from City Hall, from backstage at concert venues, and in the middle of crowds rallying for one cause or another. The reason news crews strive to produce pieces in the midst of the tumult created by a particular venue is the sense of setting.

If you want to convey a message, it's vital to create a memorable setting. I laughed when one student shared the image of her boss arriving for a meeting in a Minuteman's uniform from the Revolutionary War. He was trying to convey a message about quick response and immediacy.

Had he simply walked into the room and said, "The British are coming! And we need to be ready to respond in a moment's notice," it would have been quickly forgotten in the morass of a dozen other meetings. But his uniform and the setting it created made the message powerfully memorable.

To take someone to a setting does not necessarily involve extensive costuming or remote locales. It does require the ability to set a stage with words, however. If words alone are to convey the message, they must be used in a context familiar to the audience. Simply telling the audience to "imagine you're in a very cold place" will not establish a powerful connection. Reminding the audience of a personal experience will go a long way toward ensuring audience members' actually living the experience. For example, "Think back for a moment to the last time you were caught outside on a cold, gray, dreary day, and you were soaked through to the bone. You know the kind of cold I'm talking about. The kind you simply cannot shake. When you're chilled through and just can't warm up." This way, they can become part of the setting. Setting helps make message more memorable, as the audience can go there and become an element within a greater environment.

Personal Influence

You! That's a very powerful word. But it's a word that's horribly overused and abused. Those trying to convey a message frequently ascribe traits to *you* that *you* simply doesn't have.

In the time it's taken me to write this article, I've received some e-mail indicating change in my life:

- "You can get the lowest fixed rate on a mortgage."

- "You can make massive profits on eBay."

- "Your partner will love you for this."

I don't think so.

The word *you* is assigned to us without consideration of whether you really feel a particular way. People are not influenced by what is expected of them with a flash of the word *you*. They are influenced, however, when their true, personal needs are identified, assessed, and addressed. There's a connection between parties in the communication process when you can find a personal need, a desire, or an understanding that reflects what the listener is thinking. This is why some talk-show hosts are phenomenally successful. They echo what the listener is thinking. If you can identify the needs of listeners and connect with them, there's a lot of value.

One other e-mail came in with the barrage cited earlier. It was from one of the major chain department stores, announcing its "Summer Sale Spectacular" on slacks and shorts. It came in screaming, "Your chance to save on slacks!"

Last night, while flying home from Atlanta, I tore a gaping hole in the seat of my pants when they caught on the armrest of my airline seat. That chain store made an e-sale. Why? Because it happened to connect to a very personal need. The store was talking directly to someone who could identify with what it was promoting.

Sometimes, it's just luck when we connect. But if we invest the time in getting to know our team members more intimately and make ourselves familiar with their experiences and needs, personal influence can become a defining element of our interpersonal and project communications.

Woven together, these three elements create powerful communications. Not through volume or expense or rehearsal, but through a clear understanding of what makes messages stick.

* * *

Holiday History and a Lesson for Project Managers

Learning Some Classic Lessons about Modifying Schedules

(October 2005)

October 31 is the end of a month. On the old Celtic calendar, however, it used to be the end of the year. That was important. It was a time for closing out the concerns of the year gone by and focusing instead on a fresh start November 1. It was a time of celebrating the harvest. It was a day of acknowledging the dead as well. Catholic tradition was similar. Catholics celebrated a day of all souls in May. But they also had a conflict. They were recognizing the dead in May. The indigenous Celtic culture recognized the dead at the end of October. Pope Gregory II solved it. The Church's All Saints' Day is now November 1 (as it has been since it was moved in the eighth century). And that makes the day prior All Hallows' Eve, or Halloween.

It's more than a compelling factoid. Moving a holiday is a big deal. Imagine a suggestion to change something major, like New Year's or your country's independence day. Imagine something even more major, like moving the deliverable date for your next milestone.

The migration of All Saints' Day from spring to fall was no accident. And although there's contention over whether it was capitulation to the pagans, there was enough of an impetus for Pope Gregory II to make the move. Why would he have done such a thing? It would take a significant shift in life as we know it to make it happen. To move a date that had been established for hundreds of years would be a big deal.

In the 1930s, Franklin Delano Roosevelt (FDR) moved Thanksgiving. He did it to expand the Christmas shopping season during the Great Depression. In 1971, Richard Nixon moved Washington's Birthday from February 22 to the third Monday in February (now Presidents' Day). And Columbus Day (now Discoverer's Day in some states) moved from October 12 to the second Monday in October in 1971 as well.

Veterans Day is the classic, however. Recognizing the Armistice that ended World War I, November 11 was the official Veterans Day holiday until 1971 when it moved to the fourth Monday in October. That turned out to be temporary. Although All Saints' Day, Thanksgiving, and Presidents' Day remain moved, veterans are a force to be reckoned with. Through an intense seven-year lobbying period, they got the date moved back to where it acknowledged the true date of the Armistice, November 11. By 1978, Veterans Day was back "home."

This kind of action is significant in that it represents the tendency of organizations and individuals to want to keep dates where they are, even if it's less than expedient.

FDR learned this in the '30s. He had to make a case to move Thanksgiving, and it took years before some of the states finally went along with his seemingly bizarre scheme to move the holiday back a full week just to increase the holiday shopping season.

This ties to our project management realities when it comes to schedules and plans and deadlines. What made the successful date moves successful? What made the failures fail? Three keys seem to predominate:

- Political support

- A clear rationale

- The ability to overcome emotional ties

Political support for changing a deadline or milestone is not borne out of surprises. It's borne out of communication. It's developed through clear and effectively sharing information. Data are cultivated and presented to small audiences at first and then to larger audiences as the opportunity evolves. Data are never totally sprung on an audience. By the time data are presented to a large-base audience, there are enough nodding heads to build a bit of a bandwagon effect in getting others to acknowledge that there might be a good idea here. *Lesson 1: Get support internally early before spreading the message around. FDR, Nixon, and Gregory II did that well.*

The concept of having a clear rationale for moving deadlines means having more reasons than just it'll be better/easier. The rationale has to have benefits all the way around. The early church wrestled with opposition and an occasional appearance of weakness. Having holidays fall at the same time as the traditional local rituals fell made it easier for all parties to look as though they were part of the same faith. Nobody stood out. Everyone had a vested interest in the change. The pagans would be less likely to be persecuted. The Catholics would have the appearance of a higher level of control. FDR moved Thanksgiving because the nation was in the Great Depression, and shopping for Christmas was the major annual retail event. Nixon won with the Monday holidays because it meant the proliferation of three-day weekends, not only for federal workers but also for anyone who followed even part of the federal calendar. *Lesson 2: Find a rationale for the change that the whole body of stakeholders can appreciate.*

Perhaps the greatest challenge is overcoming emotional ties. In the Christmas classic movie *Holiday Inn,* the producers poke fun at the Thanksgiving change by having an animated turkey move back and forth across the calendar. When Nixon moved Veterans Day, the level of ownership and passion associated with the Armistice proved too great to overcome in the long term. Even arbitrarily set deadlines and milestones evoke passion. Once they're established, they take on a life of their own. Over a decade ago, one former employer had originally set a deadline date for a move two miles down the road in Washington DC. The date was set, and everyone was braced for it. When the date changed just days before the move, without warning, notice, or reason, a sense of corporate anarchy set in. Personnel were angry, and the reactions from individuals and labor unions were visceral, even though the original date had simply been arbitrarily set. Deadlines become real. Milestones have owners. People believe in them. Although we want others to believe that deadlines have meaning, if they may move, we want to soften their relationship with the dates. In another move by another employer, the original deadline was provided as a window of time, gradually narrowing to a single date within the window. The milestone for the move never became carved in granite until it was ready to be memorialized. The move's timing never came into question. *Lesson 3: If a date may move, identify the conditions under which it may move or don't provide a single hard date until you know. And if that can't be done, be* sure *Lessons 1 and 2 are applied.*

Between now and the end of the year, many project deadlines will be overcome by events. The holidays have a nasty way of doing that. If a deadline or milestone is going to be missed, be sure to learn the lessons of an ancient pope and two past presidents: communicate early and often why the date is changing; have a clear rationale for the change; and strive to minimize the emotional attachment to the date before trying to shift it.

* * *

We're All Virtually There

Using Project Management Practice to Resolve Classic Organizational Concerns in the Virtual Environment

(January 2006)

The virtual workplace. It's all around us. In fact, virtual teaming, virtual projects, and virtual environments are virtually invading our everyday lives virtually every day. But what does it mean to be truly "virtual"? And are we really managing the virtual workplace?

The challenge is not virtual; it's real. With our team members (and ourselves) at a host of remote locations, it's difficult to manage work. Indeed, more and more highly competent, qualified, and respected professionals (present company included), spend many of their days garbed in T-shirts and Chuck Taylor Converse All-Stars, sitting back on the porch with a laptop resting across their legs trying to get work done with a cat crying out for attention or the timer buzzing away on the dryer. Ahhhh ... the joys of the virtual workplace.

In days of yore, the primary distractions in the workplace were the peers in the next cube, glancing over the divider and asking for a piece of tape or a spare pushpin. Now, the distractions are the UPS man at the door, the phone call from the Friends of Things We Don't Care About Society, or the darned spot on the carpet that we've been meaning to scrub out since last April. The blessings of the virtual workplace of solitude and isolation are also its curses. They afford us the ability to truly perform. They also afford us the ability to be truly distracted.

So how can we best manage virtual work? The painfully obvious answer is one that merits a spot on the Project Management Professional (PMP) exam: it's project management. When you think about the basic practices of good, effective project management, they are born for inclusion in the day to day of the virtual workplace. Specifically, a few project management best practices are *very* best practices in the virtual workplace. They include the following:

- Management by objectives (MBO)

- Decomposition

- Thresholds and tolerances

- Team rules and guidance

Management by Objectives
In the virtual environment, it's very easy to drift from one mission to another without a clear sense of accomplishment or a sense of mission. Clear objectives afford both. In dealing with virtual teams, however, crafting objective upon objective can be a time-consuming prospect. As an alternative, consider having virtual team members define their own objectives, bringing them to you for validation and

acceptance or approval. Ensure that such objectives meet the SMART criteria of being specific, measurable, agreed upon, realistic, and time constrained. If they do, we can then allow for a measure of self management and independence in an environment that requires those behaviors.

Decomposition

A close cousin to MBO is the work breakdown structure practice of decomposition of work. Breaking work down into logical, manageable components makes sense in any project. It makes twice the sense when you're trying to ensure that those in the remote environment have a clear sense that they're making headway and that they feel upbeat and positive about their role in projects.

By identifying discrete pieces of work and doling them out to the appropriate individuals, there's a chance for team participants in those remote locations to mark work as "complete," without necessarily completing massive chunks of the project. In the remote environment, small, discrete components of work open the doors for accomplishment. Because the work in the virtual team often means a lack of communication or understanding, the only communication that sometimes happens is the handoff of deliverables. If those deliverables can be rendered more discrete, then it becomes possible to increase the levels of both accomplishment and communication.

For the individual members of the team, smaller pieces of work mean they can offer more regular contributions to the project. It allows them to participate more frequently and to provide management a sense that they regularly and significantly contributing to the project.

For management, smaller pieces of work mean we have the ability to manage specific deliverables without the appearance that we are micromanaging the individuals. By simply getting status updates on the individual work elements, we get a clearer sense of remote activity and regular indicators that those in remote locations are engaged in work that contributes to the project as a whole.

Thresholds and Tolerances

Setting down thresholds and tolerances is one way of making life in the virtual world just a little more real. By sharing insights on what is an acceptable behavior and what's not, we establish the norms common to nonvirtual work. In most traditional workplaces, we readily have a sense of when we're stretching the boundaries of acceptable behavior. In the virtual workplace, those boundaries have to be spelled out more explicitly. If we provide information to team members about when, how, and why to escalated concerns and when to deal with them on their own, they are truly empowered to act as effective virtual employees. Failure to do so encourages the situation in which team members are saddled with the burden of establishing their own norms and then discovering whether their assessments were accurate.

Simply telling virtual employees "If you get more than one call from the customer in a given day, let me know" will go a long way toward clarifying what's a normal behavior and what's not.

Team Rules and Guidance

Did you ever play the board game MONOPOLY in an unfamiliar household? It's interesting. Despite the fact that the rules of the game are carefully detailed in the standard rulebook, every family seems to play the game differently. Land on "Go," and you collect nothing or collect $200 or collect $400 or collect $500.

Different players, different rules. Normally, you don't discover these differences until a player hits the magic spot: Free Parking, Another potential social nightmare. The project environment is all the more volatile and all the more real when compared to a board game. The CEO calls in. What are the rules? A team member asks for help in doing her work. What are the rules? A customer asks for a modest change in how meetings are done. What do we do? If we can build the moral equivalent of a frequently asked questions (FAQ) document for our team members on how the team will function and what the rules of the game are, we go a long way toward accommodating the wants, needs, and understanding of our organization, and we take significant first steps toward establishing the project culture for our team members, even though they are functioning remotely.

Virtually?

Any time spent in isolation can lead to fantasy. We can have positive fantasies that we'll be able to complete the impossible tasks. We can have negative fantasies that the project will disintegrate on our watch. We can start to believe that everyone loves us or hates us. The isolation of the virtual work environment can afford some of the highest levels of potential productivity, or it can dissolve in a sea of games of solitaire or independent frustration.

As managers, it's up to us to ensure that we have a clear vision of which direction our virtual teams are taking. It's up to us to provide support and direction in ways that are meaningful. That type of team support requires no mystic capabilities or extensive leadership training. It requires simple, clear support in ways that enable team members to function more effectively when they're remotely located. That doesn't mean we have to invest huge amounts of time and energy visiting them onsite or nurturing their every action. We do, however, have to provide a framework for success and ensure that framework works.

* * *

The Next Big Project Management Thing

Examining the Value and Challenges of the Latest PM Certification: The Earned Value Professional (EVP)

(April 2006)

Carl Pritchard, EVP. See those three letters after my name? They're new. The reason they're there? I believe they're the next big project management thing. I am Carl Pritchard, Earned Value Professional.

Over the past few years, although many organizations have tried to modify project management practice to fit their needs, the U.S. federal government has begun a migration back to the basics. And that move may drive a major revival in a project management classic: earned value.

The Push for Earned Value

The Office of Management and Budget's Circular No. A-11, Section 300, sets the standard for government information technology (IT) projects and now has a requirement for earned value management systems (EVMS) that comply with the American National Standards Institute (ANSI) standard. The actual language regarding EVMS for major IT projects is clear. Projects that want to be in the top tier for federal funding consideration must meet these criteria: Agency will use, or uses an Earned Value Management System (EVMS) that meets ANSI/EIA Standard 748 and project is earning the value as planned for costs, schedule, and performance goals.

Exhibit 300 calls for clarification of what types of earned value practices are being used. What this governmentese means is that government project managers are expecting projects to adhere to best practice EVMS procedures. How do you know whether you're compliant with ANSI/EIA Standard 748? Ask a professional.

It's not all a government-project phenomenon. On the commercial side of the house, many organizations are wrestling with the challenges of complying with Sarbanes–Oxley's requirements for "internal controls." (For those unfamiliar with Sarbanes–Oxley [SOX], it's the government regulation that requires publicly traded companies to have clear controls on how and why they are investing in what they're investing in. It was created in the wake of the Enron scandal.) In the April 2004 issue of *Contract Management,* Quentin Fleming and Joel Koppelman assert that the only truly effective way to apply internal controls is through the effective application of earned value (Fleming 2004). Up until now, there's been no single recognized means for validating capability in earned value. But in June 2005, that changed. That's when the Association for the Advancement of Cost Engineering (AACE, www.aacei.org) introduced the Earned Value Professional exam.

Requirements to Become an Earned Value Professional

Much like the Project Management Professional (PMP) exam, the prerequisites for EVP are a history of work in the profession and the résumé to support that history. The major difference, however, is the expectation that someone applying for the EVP should have the breadth of understanding of the insights associated with the ANSI standard for earned value (Earned Value Management Systems, ANSI/EIA 748).

Again, as with the PMP, there is an exam associated with the certification, but the certification exam is slightly different, and it's broken into four parts.

Part 1: The first part of the exam is a test on the fundamentals of project management. Although it is based on the *Skills and Knowledge* guidance (a textbook published by AACE), the questions and approaches associated with this section should not prove overly daunting for anyone who has already sat for the PMP. The hour and a half allotted for this section of the test is generous.

Part 2: The second part of the exam is a classic set of earned value math problems. Most of the questions here are strictly math drills, and as long as the test taker knows and understands the math associated with earned value, again, this section is not too difficult. One note is that AACE still sticks with the standard earned value terms as applied in the U.S. federal environment, which means that earned value is referred to as the budgeted cost of work performed (BCWP), and the planned value is referred to by its classic name of budgeted cost of work scheduled (BCWS). As long as those terms are familiar and the math is in one's comfort zone, this component of the exam is not a major problem.

Lunch break: Just a note about the lunch break. As neither of the first two sections requires too much time or mental energy, the lunch break is a quiet, self-satisfying moment. Don't take it as such. If you haven't invested enough time in truly understanding the details of ANSI/EIA 748, this is your last chance to tackle them.

Part 3: If Parts 1 and 2 didn't test your mettle, Part 3 will definitely make up for it. This is the heavy lifting on this exam, with plenty of esoteric questions about the nature of the work hour, the options for claiming techniques (how and when to claim completion for a task), and the appropriate time for the appropriate technique. If there is a section that forces work through both challenging math and interpretation of that math, this is definitely it. This section requires the full hour and a half to complete.

Part 4: Part 4 also takes the full hour and a half, but in this instance, it's time that feels phenomenally well spent. Why? It's an essay test. AACE cleverly developed an extensive earned value spreadsheet that addresses virtually every potential scenario one could have on a given project and then asks you to craft a management memo explaining the past, present, and future of the project. It's a fair and honest assessment of one's ability to read the tea leaves of earned value. The advantage for this section will go to those who can both understand earned value and express themselves effectively in a management memorandum in the first draft. The ability to craft an idea, cope with writer's cramp, and interpret earned value all at the same time pays off in this exam component.

So Why Bother with Another Certification?

The EVP is currently in its infancy. Its evolution may determine the future course of both government and commercial practice in earned value. And with the government emphasis on earned value through the Office of Management and Budget and through Sarbanes–Oxley, there is a distinct possibility that—strategically planned or otherwise—earned value may find its way into your future.

As a professional, project managers have options. They may assume that earned value is not on the horizon for them, or they can become early adopters of the certification. By doing so, they put themselves in a position where they can be pioneers of a practice and the first of a new generation of project management leaders.

* * *

It's 2006, and You're Not Certified?

Looking at the Value and Challenges of Life without Certifications

(June 2006)

Good for you. Seriously, I mean it. If you've made it through the past two decades without earning a certification of some stripe, you've actually accomplished a great deal. That's no mean feat. Organizations ritually demand that their personnel become certified in one practice or another, and the challenge for many employees is that although they are the best in the business at what they do, they may not have the time, energy, or capability to be certified. But how do you sell it? How do you sell the notion that you're a competent professional if you're not MCSE , or PMP, EVP, CPA, CFP, or MBA? How do you prove that you're just as good as, if not better than, the next professional?

Let me toss out one more set of initials for you: CV, curriculum vitae, your professional life story, your résumé. A PhD friend of mine sent along his CV for an award he was applying for recently. It was amazing. It was (and I'm not making this up) thirty-six pages long. I read through it page after page. There was a staggering volume of information about his accomplishments, projects completed, groups led, articles written, publications accepted, and a professional life well lived. It was inspired (if not more than just a little too long). Near the top of his list were more than half a dozen certifications, ranging from the CPE (Certified Professional Estimator) to the Level II CPM (Certified Program Manager) certification issued by the DoD (Department of Defense). But those said little, if not nothing, without the ream of paper that followed. The paper that followed included detail on courses taught, organizations led, and roles and honors bestowed.

The detail after the certifications should matter, but for many organizations, the list of abbreviations and acronyms seem to make the difference.

How do we overcome that? It's a challenge to say the least. I myself pursue certifications just to justify myself and to level the playing field with those who wonder whether I'm really up to the task of serving the organizations I serve. But some professionals frankly shouldn't have to. They have the background, history, and skills that represent some of the best and brightest our profession has to offer. Because they haven't had the time or inclination to chase a given certification, I don't believe they should inherently be written off as lesser professionals. Instead, I believe that CVPMs (curricula vitae project managers) or CRPMs (crucible of reality project managers) merit high praise and note. The challenge comes in getting management and others in the organization to recognize the inherent value of these noncertified individuals. Thus, for these individuals, it's important to get a shared understanding of what the certificate is supposed to represent and accomplish. What does management want from the certification? What are the goals for certified personnel? If the goals are to have meaning, they should not hinge exclusively on a formal credential. They should hinge on performance. They should hinge on the organization's capacity to benefit from that performance.

So what are the benefits of the PMP certification? What are the benefits of MCSE certification? What are the benefits of the EVP certification? Different organizations have different perspectives on the value added by the certifications. For some organizations, it's a function of having credible professionals to add to RFPs. For others, it's a matter of being able to show subject matter expertise. For still others, it's fundamental bragging rights. The challenge is figuring out what the real objective of the organization is and how it can be served.

Certification Alternatives

What's as good as a certification? A degree, for one thing. Although certifications show currency and an effective understanding of the latest and greatest, a degree shows a comprehensive body of understanding. All too often, organizations discount the intensity of the collegiate experience. In many cases, individuals get specialized training, and that specialization is forgotten over time or obscured by a general description (like BS, engineering). We need to reinforce the special training and special nature of our education and ensure that those who seek expertise know that we are available to flex that expertise.

What else measures up? Publications, articles, paper presentations, conference roundtables, specialized business experiences, charitable efforts of significance.

Also, don't discount business titles. Vice president? Chief information officer? Executive director? Executive associate? In one position I held, I explained to my boss that I wanted my business cards to read "Utility Infielder." He refused. He explained that the organization would get far more leverage out of my position as director. If the organization wants us to look more impressive, it can be a wonderful opportunity to lobby for an enhanced title. Who would you rather have supporting your project? A PMP or an SD (senior director)? Granted, those in the project management know might contend that a PMP would be more valuable, but the cultural realities often dictate that title trumps certification.

First Steps

So if you're not oriented toward another professional certification exam, it is time to enhance your professional image. Consider all the possibilities that might be driving the organizational push for certification, and ask the question "what's the outcome they want?" Effective management teams will have an answer. Ask what options build the types of leverage they seek, and pursue them. Look at the possibilities of how to enhance your professional status and where those possibilities may take you. And start down that road.

* * *

Droughts, Dry Spells, and Summer Rains

Coping with the Inevitable Shortages: Being Ready and Knowing the Implications of the Inevitable

(August 2007)

In our area of the East Coast of the United States, as well as in other spots around the globe, summer's heat took its toll, leaving parched lawns, shriveled fruit, and pathetic-looking new plantings from the spring. The blazing sun has taken its toll with weeks of 90+ temperatures and zero precipitation. Almost every summer has a period like this in our area, and each year people inevitably throw around the *D* word: *drought.* As I studied my dying new bushes and paltry tomato crop, I was able to reflect back five years and remember a true drought. It was a stretch of dry weather that lasted for almost a year rather than weeks, slaughtering all but the hardiest of plants. The *Random House Dictionary* definition for *drought* is interesting: "1. a period of dry weather, esp. a long one that is injurious to crops; an extended shortage." That differs from a *dry spell*, which gets its own definition: "a prolonged period of dry weather; a period of little or no productivity or activity, low income, etc." (Random House 1987).

As two days of substantial rain draw to a close, I'm left with the impression that despite my fear and trepidation, we're in the midst of a dry spell rather than a drought. What's the distinction? A drought leaves you with real physical harm. A dry spell is a nuisance that makes you paranoid you're heading for a drought. No one can truly sufficiently prepare for a drought. There are not enough rain barrels on the planet to cope with a shortage that lasts for major portions of a year or years. But there are enough rain barrels to get you through a dry spell.

This metaphor is appropriate when it comes to shortages on our projects. Those may include shortages of cash, of human resources, of political capital, of client goodwill, or of almost any project commodity. We suffer from regular encounters with dry spells and, fearing droughts, react in pained dismay. Our challenge is distinguishing between the two, both in terminology and in action.

As the risk guy, I'm a firm believer that we can do a better job of labeling these problems to steel ourselves appropriately for drought or dry spell and be willing to make distinctions between the two. Specifically, it's a function of warning those around us of current conditions and getting their interpretation of the signs in the environment. To brace ourselves appropriately, we need to establish the right environment and communicate the implications of changes to that environment.

The Dry Spell Warning System

National and state parks in fire-prone areas often have a wood plaque that reads: "Today's Fire Danger Is ..." The terms that follow are generally *low, moderate, high, very high,* and *extreme.* Each term has meaning to the National Weather Service. Very high means it doesn't take much to start a fire. Extreme means almost any ignition source could set the area ablaze. Some things you simply don't do once you get above moderate. You don't host a barbeque in the forest. You don't engage in risky behaviors.

We can set up similar systems for our own dry spells. By letting team members and management know when we're going to shift to lower consumption rates and less risky behavior, we also communicate when we have the potential for serious trouble because of the shortage associated with the commodity in question.

For resources (human or material), we can set the following criteria:

- Low concern might exist when all resources are available and at our disposal.

- Moderate might stand when resources are available but conflicts potentially limit their ongoing availability.

- High might exist when they are currently overassigned or overcommitted.

- Very high could be when their availability to our projects is already reduced, very limited, or in decline.

- Extreme may exist when less than 50 percent of resources are available versus what's needed.

For political capital, we can set the following criteria:

- Low concern might exist when the project is popular with all available stakeholders.

- Moderate might stand when the project is perceived favorably, but some of the stakeholders have concerns about the team or project performance.

- High might exist if there are distinct groups that are opposed to the project, the approach, or the performers.

- Very high could be when such groups are already vocal and active.

- Extreme may exist when there are virtually no supporters of the project in the body of stakeholders.

Note that we could establish criteria for almost anything and establish the points to watch as the project progresses from low to moderate to high (or improves from high to moderate to low). The beauty of such systems is that they clarify what constitutes a trend or change. If we're going from low to moderate, we might advise management that we have a shared understanding that their support may be helpful in keeping the project from "flaming out." They may be able to provide support by increasing the resources or providing moral support.

From Dry Spell to Drought
With dry spells, it's a matter of predicting future behavior. With droughts, it's a matter of time to recover. It's not a risk, it's an issue—a risk that has come to fruition. It's a whole different state of being.

What issues can drive us to formally be in a drought? Stream levels, precipitation, reservoir levels, groundwater levels, or soil moisture can all provide the warning signs. On these, just as the weather forecasters can tell you what it might take to overcome a drought, in our project environments, we should be looking for what it will take for us to overcome an existing problem.

What problems might serve as evidence of a project drought?

- Resource levels

- Stakeholder reaction

- Schedule delays

- Cost variance

As issues managers, we can respond when the expenditure of resources, political capital, or community goodwill hits crisis levels. Before it ever happens, we ask what would we do if the worst-case scenario happened? For community goodwill, for example, what would we do if we wound up as pariahs in the local media? If we establish our contingency strategies for the areas of great concern before they come to pass, we are at least ready to take the first steps toward survival through the driest of times. And although we may not be able to completely resolve the situation, we may be able to weather the storm (or lack thereof).

The metaphor here is critical. If we know what constitutes crisis levels and how we'll react, then we know when we're still in trouble and when the crisis has passed. In my community of Frederick, Maryland, 2001–2002 was our drought year. From early '01 until August '02, dry weather prevailed, prompting building moratoriums and calls for severe water restrictions. From August through January '03, the clouds broke forth and the rains came and came and came. On February 21, 2003, the almost comical headline "Drought Rules Lifted as Flooding Looms" appeared in the *Frederick News-Post*. As project managers, we need to be sufficiently proactive to ensure that we not only know what we'll do to respond but also how we'll know it's time to declare victory and move beyond our concerns. That's when we've truly mastered the challenging art of "drought management." If we know what constitutes trouble, we also should inherently understand what constitutes success over those troubles. In Frederick, it became a running joke (as the floodwaters rose) that the drought might someday end. As project managers, we are truly successful not only when we plan for the worst but also when we know when the worst has passed.

* * *

PROCESS: CONTROLLING

Did Somebody Say Customer Service?

*Looking at the Role of the Project Manager (and Every Team
Member in the Overall Project Experience for Our Internal
and External Customers)*

(July 2000)

Project managers have a compelling duality (or triality) of
roles on projects. One of the key roles is ensuring customer
service throughout the project experience. It's a critical
risk area and one that's often overlooked. Shortly after he
wrote his landmark book *The Service Edge*, by Ron Zemke
and Dick Schaaf, Dick Schaaf and I had the occasion to talk
(Zemke 1990). He emphasized the need for corporate entities
to recognize a service strategy. And the strategy must be
deployed consistently at all levels.

As project managers for our organizations, we represent
one of the critical levels of customer service. We have direct
contact with the customer. We have supervisory responsibility
for our resources. We produce product. We have direct
contact with upper (or functional) management. All these
contacts represent both risk and opportunity. They represent
risk in terms of potential failure points in customer service,
and they represent opportunities in terms of being able to
establish more positive customer relations. We do this in an
environment where our direct authority is extremely limited,
which can put us in a somewhat tenuous position.

Toward that end, there are a handful of basic customer
service rules and roles that we can heed along the way to
improve both the customer's experience and our own.

Customers see what we enable them to see. The service manager in a recent service experience regaled me with lengthy explanations about how my appointment was lost, how his department does this all the time, and how I should make sure I get the appointment taker's name next time. He "squeezed me in," nonetheless. I would have thought the process flawless had he simply excused himself, checked on process/system availability, and incorporated me in the schedule. Customers don't need (or necessarily want) to see our internal concerns. If we want the image of high performance, we must generate that image at all steps in the process.

Everyone has to know what constitutes quality. A single team member nay-saying the organization can be potentially lethal to customer service. But team members need to vent. Reinforce that you are the point of contact for all such venting, not the customer or the customer's representatives.

The product has to live up to the image. Deliverables must reflect the same level of quality that the team and the management do. In some cases, this may force the customer into a position of reestablishing what constitutes quality. If time or budget constraints cannot be met without sacrificing quality, it's important to allow the customer to participate in the decision-making process. As project managers, we are not the sole arbiters of quality. A Halloween mask completed on November 4 is not a quality product. Even if it's beautiful, it wasn't there in time to serve the customer's needs. If you are not sure which side of the triple constraint the customer would most willingly surrender, make sure you find out.

Why the drumbeat on customer service? It's risk. And it's a risk we can readily deal with. We have direct control. We have the ability to ensure that the team knows how the customer will be treated. We have the ability to create demarcations between what's acceptable and what's not in terms of team behavior around the customer. We have the ability to drill toward a consistent message of how to communicate with the customer and ensure that the customer's needs are met (and met well).

* * *

A Summer Break from Risk?

The Value of Taking a Second Look at Risk without Weighing It Down with Process

(April 2001)

Just a few short weeks and summer will officially be upon us. Vacations. Time with family and friends. More BBQ, less work. And so risk takes a vacation, right? Unfortunately, no. In its own insidious fashion, risk continues to grow, fester, and take hold within our projects. It's just not fair. Nevertheless, it is reality. But is there merit to taking a summer break from all the worry and fret associated with our projects? Perhaps. It's a matter of how we take that break. Specifically, we take a break, and for a short season let our processes do the work.

Carl, that sounds a bit idealistic, doesn't it? Let the process do the work? I don't know that that will work in my environment. If I'm not beating the "risk drum," there's no one marching to it.

Then I contend that you aren't letting the processes function in the way in which they're intended, or worse, there are no rigorous risk processes in place. Ideally, we should have the situation in which, at the beginning of our projects, we identified the risks. We logged them well. We flagged them and tagged them according to their causes within the work breakdown structure. We have created the infrastructure so that everyone in the project has a common vision about what constitutes a moderate impact and what constitutes a high impact. We have identified the work responsible to deal with the best responses. And we have added the appropriate activities to the structure. What's left to do?

For the summer break, the process should be self-sustaining. If a customer places a change order, risk will be evaluated based on that change. If disaster strikes, team members will react based on the responses we've identified. They'll escalate when the risk triggers indicate that it's time to escalate. They'll know when to buzz you at the beach because you have a common vision about which risks are mission critical and which can ostensibly be placed on the back burner.

Notice that we haven't abandoned risk. We're just letting the processes function. And we're cutting ourselves some slack.

Some of you have already caught on. This isn't just a summer thing. It's a pattern of good behavior on risk. It's a process that, when it's taken hold, allows us to build in some freedom from the frenzy of the project and the chaos brought on by a lack of control. We're building control into the project. And that's the very nature of the risk process. If we build it in, and inculcate it into the day-to-day activities, we buy ourselves freedom. We buy ourselves an increased level of comfort in our management activity. But the key is that we don't run this process alone. We do it with others working on our side, in our best interests, and adhering to the process. If we can achieve that, we've made enormous strides toward ensuring that risk is a best practice.

* * *

It's a Beautiful Day in the (Project) Neighborhood: Forty Minutes with Fred Rogers

How Mr. Rogers Can Give Us True Power in the Communications Environment

(October 2002)

It's been more than fifteen years since I met Mister Rogers, and I still can't shake the experience. Fifteen years. He's outlasted most of my socks (which my lovely wife accuses me of hanging onto forever).

By way of explanation, my PPM (preproject management) career was in radio. I was the news director of WASH-FM, Washington DC, in the '80s. It's a rather labyrinthine career path I'll delve into some other time. But one of my roles was to do author interviews. Celebrities hawking their latest books would cross my doorstep in a flurried rush to get one more bit of publicity before getting out of Washington. This day, it was to be Mister Rogers.

I did my traditional rushed introductions as I set up the equipment in the studio. As I strung sentence after sentence together in a blurt of verbal diarrhea, Fred Rogers leaned across the table and spoke in his gentle voice. "Please don't rush on my account. We have a full forty minutes together. I want to make sure you get everything you need."

It was eerie.

Just as I had watched him calm my son with gentle voice and soothing tone, he was doing the same for me. But there was something more. It was focus. The man was focused, and he was focused on me. The more he spoke, the more he talked about what I hoped to get from the interview and how I could take best advantage of our time together. He was interested in ensuring I looked good. In my years of conducting such interviews, no one had ever done that for me. He wasn't worried about his next limo ride, his interview upstairs at Channel 5, or his agenda for the Minneapolis leg of the trip. He was focused on me.

The interview went well, with the traditional give-and-take of information about his philosophy, attitude, and approach to life. As he spoke, I gave each concept greater weight because of the deference he had shown me. I lent him more credence because he had done the same for me. And when he left, I found I had turned into a fan of Mister Rogers, explaining his positions to others and identifying why he's such a great influence for children.

My children have now outgrown Mister Rogers. I have not. I believe he has a powerful message for project managers and particularly project managers in charge of sizeable teams. It's a message of respect and focus, two traits we can leverage as project managers to higher levels of performance and more dedicated teams.

Respect

Respect is not just a lip-service acknowledgement of a person's accomplishments. It is, according to *Chambers Dictionary of Etymology* (Barnhart 1999), rooted in the Latin terms for "regard, delay, and look back." It comes from stopping and looking at something or someone. It didn't turn to mean honor or deference until the mid-1550s. Mister Rogers seems to know that lesson all too well. In dealing with his tour hosts, he showed them respect. When they asked a question or posed a concern, he paused, considered their issue, and provided a thoughtful response. Position or title did not appear to be the roots of his interest. He seemed to genuinely respect them as peers.

As project managers, we fight the occasional battle to set ourselves apart because of the sometimes daunting nature of our work. We sometimes strive to ensure that others understand just how complex and overwhelming our worlds can be. Rather than elevate others (be they project managers or team members), we occasionally find ourselves in a battle of "worsts," trying to outdo the other person with the challenges of our day-to-day existence.

I have three meetings this week, and two of them are out of town.

Three meetings? I have four, and for one, I'll be up at 2 a.m. for an Australian telecon.

I have four today. And the one's an all-nighter to develop a new strategy on meeting protocols.

This doesn't show a lot of respect for what each of us is going through, and I doubt Fred Rogers gets caught in this kind of battle. Respect means acknowledging what others are challenged by and attempting to show a reasonable level of empathy for their experience. It means giving them credit for what they're accomplishing and how they're accomplishing it.

Focus

This all ties in to the nature of focus. When I met with Fred Rogers, I expected a traditional celebrity experience. Celebrities expect the world to be focused on them. Most of those in the public eye that I have had the honor to meet had rather egocentric perspectives on reality. The role reversal with Fred Rogers caught me off guard. I did not expect to have him ask me what I needed or how he could help me in the course of the interview.

Similarly, most of our team members are accustomed to our propensity for multitasking. They do not expect us to have the time or energy to invest in them, even when we carve out a few minutes to have them into our offices or cubicles. We can change how much we accomplish in those little meetings and how they're received by a simple change in protocol.

Try this the next time someone asks for a few minutes of your time. Ask for fifteen seconds to prepare your desk or office. Turn off the computer monitor and the speakers. Put the phone on do-not-disturb mode or off the hook. Clear any potentially distracting papers from the desk. Grab a pen and pad for notes (and only for notes). Look across the desk. Begin the conversation.

The change in tone from the conventional office meeting will be dramatic. Those who genuinely need your time and attention will feel valued, appreciated, and recognized. They will sense the level of acknowledgement you're affording them. In many instances, they will intensify their focus to optimize your time together. By contrast, those who seek simply to shoot the breeze will sometimes be intimidated by the level of intimacy created by this practice. They will often cut short those conversations. Either way, you're improving business communication, showing respect and focus to those who merit it, and encouraging clarity of communication and information sharing.

For most project managers, multitasking has become such a way of life that to do otherwise is a major change in practice. But by becoming a little more like Fred Rogers, we have the potential to render it a more beautiful day in the (project) neighborhood.

* * *

I'll Get Those Priorities to You Tomorrow, But First

Establishing Game Plans for Dealing with Planned and Crisis Priorities

(March 2003)

Priorities. What comes first? Really? In project portfolio management, the first priorities are supposedly those that are the most important to the organization. That lasts until the first fires begin. In teaching a managing multiple projects course (online) for the Project Management Institute, we talk a lot about how to establish both formal and informal priorities and what it would take for issues to supersede those priorities.

I got a taste of my own medicine last week when a friend told me to check out the front page of my corporate Web site (emphasizing that he hadn't done it). Expecting to see my own smiling visage, I was instead surprised to find the words "you've been hacked" staring up at me, along with some pretty threatening language. Depressing stuff. The article I was working on? Forgotten. The proposal that was due to a client the next day? Secondary. What suddenly became the only thing I had to do was to report, clean out, and restore my office Web site. Nowhere on my priorities list had I included "Web site crises" as an issue or even a weight, but suddenly it had taken the front burner (and most of the rest of the stove).

Now that life is back to a relative sense of normalcy, thanks to my webmaster (Chris), I've been trying to figure out how I could have put that on my priority radar without overemphasizing what I hope was a one-time event. Crises do belong on the radar, but it gets down to ensuring we aren't saving the bathwater while the baby gets away.

Crisis Prioritization

All organizational and personal prioritization scales differ, so it's not possible to ascribe a single set of one-size-fits-all numbers to any process of this ilk. What is possible, however, is to define the way in which crisis priorities can be integrated with standard organizational priorities to validate, yet again, whether we're working on the right things first.

For crises, there are two basic considerations: urgency and impact. How quickly will this become a major disaster? How much of a major disaster does this crisis constitute?

The impact to my business of a single day of Web site loss is nominal. The impact of a week or more could become a serious blot on my client image. A month or more could cost long-term business. Note that the urgency is really not there for a first-day fix. But if allowed to continue, this problem escalates dramatically over time, undermining confidence in the organization. So how quickly does it have to be fixed?

Most clients will understand a one- or two-day outage on a corporate Web site. As such, the first triage that was done after the crisis arose should have indicated that any other pressing deadlines (like the proposal due the following day) should have taken priority. But because crises loom large and seem insurmountable, they often shove more pressing work out of the way.

One student organization prioritizes its projects as 1-, 2-, and 3-class, with 3-class being the most important and pressing. Because crises exist on a different plane of reality (sudden, immediate, unplanned), I might suggest that crises should be on the half scales at 0.5, 1.5, 2.5, 3.5. That identifies clearly which projects must occur before the crisis is resolved and which must wait. It also affirms that we (as project managers) don't have to make the call between project and crisis without some guidance.

For that scale, let me offer my thoughts on the gradient levels:

- 3.5—urgent and high impact: Ideally, the impact scales would mirror those laid out for a risk qualification scheme, but if not, these impact scales would include those that involve direct impact to human life, loss of standing as a corporation or organization, or permanent damage to the corporate entity. Urgent would be defined as those crises that, if not resolved immediately, will exacerbate the impact, or as those crises showing the full brunt of the impact is already in force.
- 2.5—urgent and moderate impact or pressing and high impact: Although the high-impact scale would remain the

same, moderate impacts are those that would be visible to the customer base and paint the organization in a significantly less favorable light. Pressing would be defined as those crises that may not suffer from a one- or two-day lapse in correction, but any long-term delay will exacerbate the situation.

• 1.5—nonurgent with high impact, pressing with moderate impact, or urgent with low impact: Here, the only change is that low impact means those that are felt internally, but are not readily visible outside the organization. Nonurgent indicates that a significant amount of time may lapse before the situation begins to escalate (which makes you wonder whether it was a crisis to begin with).

• 0.5—nonurgent or pressing with low impact: Normally, these crises exist only in the eyes of those who identify them.

When I first discovered the hacker's handiwork, I was in four-alarm, call-out-the-trucks mode. I was on the phone with the state police cybercrimes unit and spent a significant chunk of my day discussing strategy with some individuals I considered Web savvy. A critical, time-sensitive proposal on my desktop would have to wait. Although that proposal was a 3 as a business priority, the urgency of the hack pushed it off my projects list temporarily.

In retrospect, the crisis I faced was, at worst, a 2.5 on this crisis scale, and, as such, I should have taken stock and invested my afternoon in the proposal, where I belonged. Yes, the Web site is an important component of business, but, no, it was not more important than that particular project.

If the same thing happened to my personal Web pages, the crisis scale might drop to 1.5, despite my frustration with the experience. If the same thing happened to Amazon or eBay, it would definitely qualify as a 3.5 all-hands-on-deck kind of experience.

All too often prioritization models do not consider crises, assuming that the models will speak for themselves in terms of identifying which work has to come first. Without the capacity to address crisis priorities, most of the prioritization models that exist will come up short in the intense glare of the next short-term disaster, waiting in the wings.

* * *

A Renaissance for Followership

Competencies to Be a Good Follower: Looking at the Other Side of the Management Equation

(June 2004)

Now more than 330,000 project management professionals. Project management tools selling like hotcakes. Leadership remains a business concept of high value and high renown. It's hard to look at the top business book list today without seeing the words *lead, leader,* or *leadership* in at least half the titles. We're trying to breed a generation of project leaders.

But what of the project followers?

A participant in a recent keynote address actually raised that specter for me the other day. His question seemed simple enough, "Do you know of any good training for followers?"

"Team building?" I queried.

"No, just followers. I just need something to tell my team members about what it takes to be a good follower."

Sounds like a simple enough premise, but it's actually surprisingly complex. What are the objectives of good followership? What does it require? What special competencies should we look for in followers, and how can we promote them?

In informal polls of project peers, I began to explore what traits make the perfect follower. Here are the first five follower competencies that I identified and what traits should we look for in trying to find the best followers:

- Order discrimination

- Reporting propriety (when, what, and how)

- Fellow follower support

- Strategic inquiry

- Proud humility

Each of these competencies is crucial to effective followership, and each has the added bonus of setting up followers effectively for a future as either follower or leader. Leaders who can't exhibit effective followership traits will inevitably fail at nurturing effective followers because they don't know what to expect of them.

Order Discrimination
"I need you to meet with the client next Tuesday." That sounds like a simple enough request. But is it a request? Or an order? That's not an easy question to answer. In some cases, it may be something that is desired but not mandated. In other instances, in may be a simple, direct mandate. WWEFD? What would an effective follower do? When in doubt, ask. But before asking, the effective follower will assess the potential impact or influence on the body of his work.

Requests and orders are both made with the intent of influencing behavior. If there's no impediment to the follower's work, the answer should be a simple sure followed by clarification on the nature of the request. Are there implications? Of course. Followers often subvert their effectiveness by expending political capital challenging the need for their participation or presence before they've even assessed their own workload or the nature of their participation in the request's outcome. They may argue for the sake of minimizing workload, even when the workload is not overly onerous.

Although the default setting must be affirmative, the effective follower (if overloaded), may assess the workload and determine whether the meeting will be a potential impediment to other work. If that's the case, the approach that will best serve everyone is to explain that there are numerous other activities to be considered and to scope out the nature of the management mandate. The key throughout this process (outlined in the figure that follows) is support. Management loves a cheerful, solutions-oriented follower. This means identifying the hiccups before they happen and clarifying when their requests might have unexpected consequences. And it means that when the work is doable, followers just clarify their involvement and do it.

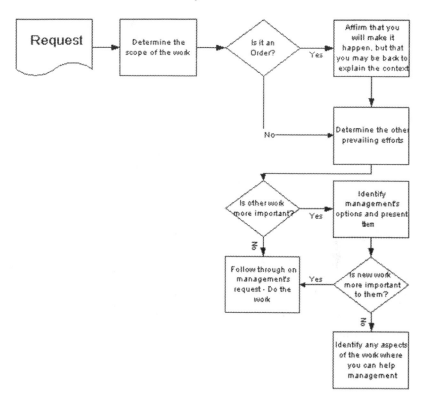

Dealing with Requests and Orders

Perhaps the most remarkable notion here is that there's not that much difference between an order and a request, save that an order is followed immediately by affirmation that the team member will perform the work. That's no small notion. Anyone who has led a team knows the challenge associated with trying to deal with team members who feel compelled to negotiate every single task assigned. It can be a draining experience for both the leader and the follower.

Reporting Propriety

When is it time for a follower to report? When

- Catastrophes might happen

- Problems appear imminent

- Followers have a concern they can't resolve

- The customer stopped by asking a lot of questions

- Management stopped by asking a lot of questions

- A regulatory agency representative stopped by asking a lot of questions

Those seem obvious, don't they? Well, not necessarily. Sometimes management just has a penchant to be close to the teams. Sometimes team members have minor concerns they shouldn't escalate. Again, here, the key to effective followership is to identify management thresholds and know what management wants reports about and trusts the follower to handle. Some managers are willing to delegate huge levels of authority. Others see such delegation as tantamount to surrendering on a project. The effective follower will identify such potential pitfalls and query her management with a set of what-ifs to determine the limits.

An effective leader will lay down these boundaries without being directed, but not all leaders are effective. And sometimes, effective leaders are created only by virtue of effective followers. The correct question is not always should I notify you if ...? Instead, the question may be I'm planning to take care of this situation autonomously if it arises. Is that all right with you? That kind of question can open the door for an effective discussion on the need for management reporting and the need for clear, distinct thresholds.

Fellow Follower Support

What have you done today to make life easier for one of your peers? The goal here is not to run around telling folks have a nice day. The goal, instead, is to genuinely create an effective follower's support structure. This is not something that top-down management has historically been effective at accomplishing. Instead, it succeeds only at the grass roots and only at the hands of effective followers. Think about the last time you worked in an organization where those seemingly magical "Kum Ba Yah" moments occurred on a regular basis. These are the environments where there's a lot of mutual congratulation, mutual acknowledgement, and insider knowledge being shared. Management can't force that to happen. Good followers can. They do this by recognizing a significant element of their organizational function is to ensure that others know what they know. That doesn't necessarily mean that all team members become interchangeable, but it does mean that they share a common understanding, acceptance, and appreciation of their roles in the organization and the implications of those roles.

How do you spot this in the effective follower? He is forever sharing tricks of the trade. The effective follower is seeking opportunities to knock down roadblocks for others. The follower is thinking six months or a year ahead in terms of building deliverables that will continue to evolve even if the follower moves on to other projects (or even other organizations). To enable effective followership, the organization should allow for the hall chats, coffee klatches, and shared lunches that encourage these types of behaviors. Allow time in meetings for discussions on "Anything you found out about the customer this week that you didn't know before" and "Did any of your peers do you a nice turn this week?" (A truly great follower will acknowledge the help of his or her peers without being prompted, but a good leader will also create the environment where that can happen without its seeming out of the ordinary).

Strategic Inquiry

This is actually a competency directly taken from the Defense Systems Management College's project management competency study done during the early 1990s, but it's germane here, as well (Defense Systems Management College 1990). All these other competencies will be supported by strategic inquiry, but it's a general competency that stands on its own as well. Strategic inquiry is the ability to ask a handful of specific, probing questions that will provide mutual understanding and clarity on a variety of issues.

Most of us have seen a journalist probing an interviewee. In that role, the journalist churns through question after question and suddenly hits the one perfect question that seems to capture the heart and soul of the information she were looking for. That is classic strategic inquiry. It's the gift of hitting the right question.

How do you know whether a follower has it? Does he have a knack for asking a question that you should have thought of? Does he have the ability to capture a board range of ideas, concepts, or concerns in the nub of a single question? Does he ask questions that are repeated time and again? If so, he has wonderful skills for strategic inquiry.

Proud Humility

Okay, I'll acknowledge that it's an oxymoron. No problem there. But this final competency is truly an asset of the effective follower. She doesn't need to be in the limelight, but she is also unwilling to surrender credit when she's done a job well. False humility is a dangerous path. It can force some followers into situations in which they no longer feel comfortable taking credit for their accomplishments. It can drive some into the box where they identify themselves as ineffective. It can harm the individual and, in the long run, harm the organization.

Pride is not the root of all evil. Taken in small, appropriate doses, it's a fine personality trait for the effective follower. The effective follower does not demand attention and constant acknowledgcment, but he does take a high degree of pride in his ability to deliver and perform. There's nothing wrong with saying I did that well, and it contributed significantly to the project. Pride becomes a problem only when it overwhelms the message with "I am more important."

How do you find whether team members have this competency? Compliment them on honest achievement. Nothing dramatic. Nothing big. But something where they clearly achieved a goal. If they can come back with a simple thank you or I appreciate that, then they have mastered the art of proud humility. If they come back with I saved the team or shucks, it weren't nothin', then they still have some work to do. Great followers will not diminish themselves, the team, or the work that was performed.

Why Followers Matter

Despite all the literature on leadership, followers matter. They are the bricks and mortar of our project, and they ensure our success. Everyone, from the CEO through the maintenance crew is, at some point, a follower. Not all of us are always leaders, but all of us regularly serve as followers, so there's a need to review, rehearse, and reinforce our roles as followers. We should strive to make sure that these competencies are evident in those around us and in ourselves. And when we spy them in action, we should not damn them with faint praise. Instead, we should champion the follower and be sure that he knows just how deeply truly effective followership is appreciated.

* * *

What Can You Do to Push Your Organization Back to Basics?: Or, Why Advanced Critical Chain Human Resource Integration Programs Are a Work of Fiction

Learning Not to Overcomplicate Our Practices

(June 2005)

I was looking over one of the myriad catalogs I receive in the mail and noticed what appears to be a trend in project management. We're steering away from the basics. In the quest to explore project management, organizations are drifting away from the fundamentals. I spoke with a potential client recently, and was asked about the advanced training I offer. I explained that I really don't believe in advanced training because I believe a lot is lost in the quest to escape the rudiments of best practice. I stressed that by really delving into the nuances and effective practices associated with the fundamentals, organizations see higher yield. I think the potential client went with another vendor.

The trend is alarming. People don't seem to want fundamentals. If they do, they want them packaged in a tight, short package to get them over with before they launch into the advanced stuff. That's a tragedy. The fundamentals are the most engaging elements of project management. They're also the place where many organizations tend to trip in their quest for effective implementation. One of my clients is currently wrestling with an upgrade to one of the high-end project management software packages. Never mind that the organization has never built schedules well with the basic tools or recorded costs before, it wants to make the step up to something more advanced. Another client, still reeling through the maze of trying to create an infrastructure for human resource management, has decided to abandon the stand-alone versions of MS Project for the higher end Project

Server version. Members of the organization are operating under the assumption that as they learn the new tool, they'll learn the best practices.

That's not a great assumption. Best practices are generally built from the basics. Great athletes start by learning the fundamentals rather than the nuances of their sport. Great bakers don't start by learning how to create a complicated soufflé but by how to crack an egg.

One might argue that the emphasis on certification has solved a significant part of this problem. To pass the certification exams (e.g., the Project Management Professional [PMP] exam, the Earned Value Professional exam), a clear understanding of the basics is required. That's not necessarily so. With the proliferation of five-days-and-you're-loaded-for-bear precertification programs, organizations are finding ways to again circumvent the basics.

What to Do about It

At the individual level, it sometimes seems that there isn't a great deal that we can do about these types of situations. They are cultural in nature and require some senior-level support to ensure that we start with the ABCs rather than complex sentence structure. In reality, the level of influence we can exert may be surprising. We exert influence in a variety of ways: by language, by practice, and by rote.

Language is something the PMP exam drills on hard. It emphasizes the criticality of speaking PMI-ese and ensuring that all project managers share a common understanding of the terminology. We have the opportunity to drive home fundamentals by stopping the abuse of terms of art in project management. Some terms inherently invite abuse and confusion. *Risk* versus *issue*. *Plan* versus *Gantt*. *Requirements* versus *scope*. If not addressed specifically, these terms can be misused and abused. What can you do about it? When someone misuses a term, ask that person's intent. It's acceptable to seek clarification by asking do you see that as an issue that's already in play or a risk that hasn't happened yet? We get a better understanding of individual intent through that line of questioning. By simply seeking clarification on what people mean when they say something, we advance the practice.

In our day-to-day practice, we can also reinforce the best practice that is effective PM. We can ensure that schedules are built using networked activities rather than fixed dates. We can build our work breakdown structure (WBS) with consistently sized work packages and well-crafted WBS dictionaries. We can ensure that project charters are signed and readily available to all team members. Those don't generally require high-level authorization or approval. They require diligence and consistency.

If we really want to win hearts over time, we can ensure that these kinds of practices become rote behaviors. Rote behaviors are those that inherently become ingrained and almost natural. One project manager I have worked with ensures that every meeting he hosts has a thorough agenda. If someone in his group or on his team suggests a meeting to him, that person doesn't even make the pitch without submitting an agenda. It's part of his mantra, his creed, his fundamental belief system in the way project management should be done right. It may be (or seem) excessively anal-retentive, but through the years, he has brought others along to his behavior simply out of sheer deference to the way he does business.

Warning Signs

There are things to watch for organizationally. And the checklist is as easy as looking at the outline of any project management essentials program:

- Do we have a charter?

- Do we have a clear scope statement?

- Do we have management signatures on both?

- Do we have thorough functional and technical requirements signed off by all the appropriate parties?

- Has the work been broken down into a consistently structured WBS?

- Did the team participate in defining the work?

- Have we estimated and budgeted based on a thorough analysis of the work to be performed (rather than just the estimated total project duration and number of resources)?

- Have we built the schedule from a list of mutually understood activities that were defined, estimated, and networked with team input?

- Have we built a list of risks, identified the major concerns, and developed and communicated strategies to deal with them?

- Have we established the type of team we'll work with and created an environment that will support the members?

- Have we set down the parameters for quality and established how we'll monitor and ensure them?

- Have we identified any outside procurements or vendors we may need and how we'll procure them?

Any place there's a missing yes answer, there's a sign that a basic PM practice has been missed. And in case you're wondering where the checklist came from, it's largely a quick list generated from the knowledge areas of the *PMBOK* *Guide* (Project Management Institute 2008). Amazingly, even when organizations are answering no to as many as half these questions, some of their personnel suggest the need for advanced project management. That's not where the greatest yield lies in our profession. The greatest insights, productivity improvements, and practical applications come from sticking to the essentials. It's not glamorous, but it works. And there are decades of evidence from organizations that have implemented the fundamentals well.

Granted, advanced project practices have the allure of being new, exciting, and challenging. And they may hold out great promise. But getting the basics down cold is generally a powerful first step in getting to advanced.

* * *

Project Manager Authority: Look under Nonfiction

Drawing on Other Types of Authority to Truly Take Charge

(July 2005)

I have all this responsibility and no authority. Management never tells me which projects are most important. I don't know which templates I should use.

You think that's bad—I don't even get templates.

These are among the common concerns raised by project managers. I know. I hear them all the time in my classes. Students consistently express these concerns about their roles in the project process and their inability to drive change or improvement because they aren't granted the authority to do so by their managers and their organizations. I suggest that project managers who have no authority have that limitation because they often impose it upon themselves. We have myriad occasions to seize authority, but, unfortunately, we don't take hold of them. Instead, we relegate the process to others, waiting for management, the project management office, or some other authority to take the reins and tell us to move forward with a vision or an approach.

If we can find the mettle to actually take advantage of those elements of authority that really matter, we can make phenomenal inroads. Our accomplishments know few bounds.

First, Forget Formal Authority

This may be the toughest aspect of authority to release. Formal authority is such a lovely thing. It is authority granted by the organization. It is authority to control and dictate. It is the ability to hire and fire. It is weak. That's right—it's weak. Those who deploy formal authority well are those who understand that it's not the formal authority that gets them where they want to go. The formal authority is a nice support structure, but it's not the be-all and end-all.

Recently, a student complained to me about a manager who was busy micromanaging her and her personnel. She said that this individual was directive, was moving people up and down in pay grade, and was seen as a petty despot. So much so, in fact, that the student was planning to quit the organization. She's not alone—several of her peers are also ready to walk. Why? Because someone with formal authority is exercising it without considering the other types of authority that render formal authority effective. Without the other types of authority, any formal authority over the long term is moot.

With that argument in hand, I suggest that the most effective types of authority for the project manager are technical, reward, and charismatic. And because we don't get much opportunity to reward our personnel, we're down to the technical and the charismatic.

Winning Hearts—One Geek at a Time

Technical authority doesn't rely on the project manager's being the smartest person in the room. It does, however, hinge on his knowing the smartest person in the room. Technical authority means that we seize power by virtue of acknowledging where it rests and what renders it valuable. Things like project plans, the work breakdown structure, the network schedules can all grant us some measures of technical authority if we understand their use and put them to work to our advantage. If the customer throws out an unachievable date and we accept it, we are not leading. If the customer throws out an unacceptable date and we can present intelligent alternatives, we take on the mantle of authority.

It takes homework to be an authority. It takes no small measure of clairvoyance. We need to be able to predict what others around us are going to do, and how and when they're going to react. If we can leverage that insight, we gain leadership opportunities.

That would be fine, but I can't even get management to tell me which projects are the real priorities.

Who sets priorities in an organization? In most, they're ad hoc. No one sets them formally. They're set by some hidden, arcane set of rules that no one understands. In teaching students to manage multiple projects, I've worked through personal project portfolio models a dozen times. And I ensure these students know that if no one else is giving them priorities, they need to. And they need to be able to defend why their priorities are their priorities. If project managers can provide a logical, considered set of rationale as to why they're doing what they're doing, it all becomes a lot more acceptable.

The other aspect of this is that it can also serve as leadership for the organization as a whole. If the organization has never looked at portfolio models, you have the opportunity to create the pioneering set.

Charisma

How's your charisma? Really? Mine, too. I don't feel charismatic, and most of the project managers I meet would not jump into a line if it was marked "High on Charisma." We think charismatic and we think of John F. Kennedy. We think charismatic and we think of Martin Luther King, Jr. We don't think about ourselves or the project manager down the hall. But charisma is not sheer force of will. Some elements can be learned, and some are best practices in project management.

Charisma is borne out of others' desire to follow us. People want to follow when you're heading in a direction they want to go. And that means we need to understand where, how, and why our team members want to go in a particular direction. If we have that insight, we have the ability to be seen as empathetic, supportive, and of like mind. And that is awfully appealing.

How do we get there? This is the hard part. We need to listen. We need to let team members share their goals, visions, and insights. We need to cede the reins for a little while—long enough to ensure that we know what matters to them and where they'd like to ultimately go. In your next meeting, try something different. Try documenting each time someone expresses a want or need. You'll find out a lot are shared. Twenty-four hours (or a little more) later, express each person's need in a slightly reformatted way, but ensure that each person understands that you understand that it's a need. You'll find these folks are more open and that they look at you in a different light. You're sharing and understanding information in a way they haven't seen before. And because you're on the same page, they're more willing to listen to the other insights (and direction) you may have to offer.

Formulaic Leadership?

Hardly. It's not that everyone can lead well. These simple approaches can facilitate everyone's leading a little better. And it's far from dark or Machiavellian. It's an opportunity to share insights, thoughts, and approaches more effectively. It's an opportunity to get others to perceive your direction as valuable and well considered. Rather than waiting to be told we can lead, it's true leadership. It's leading by example and by understanding, and by a clear, asserted willingness to actually lead.

* * *

Technical Performance Measurement, *Mad Movies,* and the Future of Project Management

*How Current Practices Can Change
Our Perspectives on Classic Work*

(June 2006)

I recently stumbled across an ancient video (circa 1985) in our family collection of an old TV show called *Mad Movies with the L.A. Connection.* In this video, a troupe of comedians revoice and reedit classic movies with new dialog, creating an entirely different (and generally hilarious) story and plot. By way of example, the classic Shirley Temple flick *The Little Princess* is recast as a story of a young girl possessed by an evil doll. (The young girl eventually tap-dances her way to wellness).

It reminded me of the quality practice of technical performance measurement (TPM), though I may be the only person who would make that association. TPM is called out in *A Guide to the Project Management Body of Knowledge* as a risk management practice. It is designed to monitor compliance to specification and requirements in much the same way as earned value monitors compliance to cost and schedule. In fact, it's been cast as the earned value of quality. TPM adopts and adapts many of the basic practices of earned value management and reworks them to create an entirely new dimension of metrics evaluation. By setting metrics for every work package and evaluating them either in process or at completion, it allows for consistent, honest progress reporting in terms of the specifications rather than simply in terms of cost and budget. It's an inspired reapplication of an older project practice. It may also point to where project management should be looking to find best new practices. Rather than just looking at the history of our own profession, perhaps we should be looking to other practices—even other professions—to find some of the best ways to improve how we do what we do.

I believe the similarities between TPM and *Mad Movies* could be a key indicator of where the future of project management should be headed. Every business, every organization, every routine has its best practices: those that are unique to the profession and those that individuals and organizations modify to make them fit within their organizations. Earned value is adopted in some organizations applying a single value to every hour of work, no matter the pay rate of the person performing it. It is applied in other organizations using modified approaches to dealing with actuals (where they are not actually available). These are outstanding ideas if everyone who will be interpreting the data understands how they were generated and why the modified approach was applied.

But how many organizations have other forms, processes, protocols, templates, and approaches that cry out to be "revoiced"? *Mad Movies* created an entirely new tone, intent, and approach with a team of creative people recognizing how the story would work with a different audience.

Accounting has generally accepted accounting practices (GAAP), which is clearly analogous to the *PMBOK® Guide* (Project Management Institute 2008). How many accounting practices could be morphed to map to more effective project management? In the fields of journalism and editing, there are style guides and specific behaviors. In medicine, triage practices and patient monitoring procedures have been tested through the centuries.

Over the past twenty years, project management has become a highly introspective practice. The nature of the *PMBOK® Guide* has been to draw attention to standing practice and how it is applied. In the twenty years ahead, if project management is to evolve into a more effective process, it will become progressively more important to look outside the profession to other professions and organizations that have learned tricks of the trade to yield higher performance.

The winners in this race will most likely be those individuals who came to project management later in their careers, after they had the opportunity to learn another career, another approach, and another set of protocols for doing business. They will recognize that the tricks they learned in another profession—and although not a perfect match—are adaptable to the field of project management.

To expedite this process, those of us already in project management should be studying, analyzing, and parsing the processes of professions outside our own. If the client is a pharmaceutical company, don't look to its project management practices for answers; look to some of its standard protocols for preparing for clinical trials. If the client is a shipping company, the newest procedures will not be found in the project management office, but in the methodologies it applies at the loading dock. If we build an awareness of analogous practices and keep our eyes open for new and innovative ways to tweak them to work in the project world, we have the opportunity to generate truly new (and potentially *Mad*) practices.

* * *

The Demystification and Remystification of Project Management: Do We Really Need the Second Decimal?

How Much Control Is Real and Is Really Required?

(March 2007)

After a class on advanced risk this week, a student stopped by the front of the auditorium and shared one of the greatest compliments the instructor could have received. "You did a great job on that Monte Carlo stuff. I always thought it was beyond me. That was a really clear example that just made good simple sense."

What a kind and reaffirming statement. Ideally, we should shoot for this in project management. But there's a seeming effort afoot to do what I refer to as the remystification of project management.

In a recent team exchange, when I suggested our effort in spreading the project management gospel should be simplification and clarification, one team member shot back with an H.L. Mencken quote: "For every complex problem, there is an answer which is clear, simple, and wrong." I have pondered that extensively since the day my team member shared it and now feel comfortable in my own position on this. There may be clear, simple, and wrong answers, but there are also clear, simple, and correct explanations.

For the past twenty years, authors, researchers, and practitioners have been striving to make project management accessible to the masses. The titles of books published in that period provide evidence of that effort. *The Complete Idiot's Guide to Project Management, Common Sense Project Management, Project Management (The Briefcase Book Series)* are but a few.

However in the last two or three years, I've noted a shift from efforts to make project management more accessible to efforts to make it more challenging. There's a proliferation of standards (portfolio management, risk management, earned value management, and program management). There are more organizations and associations. And each of these groups seems to be creating an environment in which one is attempting to outthink the other with escalating levels of depth and complexity.

Best-practice project management is not rooted in complexity. The goal of effective PM is to simplify and clarify. The work breakdown structure (WBS)—the very core of an effective project plan—is an object lesson in simplicity. It takes work and defines it down to manageable chunks. And even there, arguments are brewing about the semantics in WBS development, the scale and scope of work packages, and the increased need for zealous adherence to progressively more complex thought in dealing with this.

The problem with the more academic approach to project management is that the true business-friendly nature of project management becomes lost in a sea of arguments about the fine-grain details. For example, consider some of my recent experiences in risk management:

- Is the Program Evaluation and Review Technique (PERT) a sound tool to gather data about durations for task estimates?

- Is it practical to do a qualitative assessment of the risk level for the project as a whole?

- Is it reasonable to quantitatively evaluate individual risks?

If you answered yes to all three, you and I share a common vision. I'm wed to the notion that almost any time you are doing more analysis of a project than you otherwise might do, it's a good thing. But I've been told recently that to share or promote such notions is heresy. Quantitative analysis is the exclusive province of whole-project analysis. Qualitative is the exclusive province of task or work package analysis. And PERT? You would think it was a four-letter word. Asking people to gather the optimistic/pessimistic/most likely durations and apply them consistently in their projects? Such a notion doesn't stand the test of statistical rigor, and without that rigor, the tool should never be promoted, let alone used, the anti-PERTers argue.

Project management is best practiced inclusively, welcoming other strategies and approaches and keeping an open mind about their application.

Once, a project manager in an organization asked me to review his work breakdown structure. His work packages were roughly six to eight hours of effort. His lowest level was activities rather than work packages. The whole thing was task oriented and organization oriented. Technically, he had broken a host of rules. But, his effort was flawless in its decomposition (there was a clear breakdown of every bit of the work). The background information in each of his work packages was dreamy. The clarity with which the elements were described could have been easily interpreted by any novice.

So was it a good WBS? Yes. It simplified and clarified the work to be performed and arranged it in a fashion that supported the organization. Some contend that because it went down to activities, it's not even a WBS anymore. Such semantic arguments are fine, but as professionals, we need to be braced for the backlash from the hardworking, real-world, in-the-trenches community.

How do we then blend the need for rigor with the need for practicality and understanding? We include. We include approaches in common accepted practice. We identify their pros and cons. We include what works, and if there's a potential limitation associated with it, we include that, too. Project offices that want to appear responsive will include new angles, approaches, and ideas along with the old ones, as long as they won't harm the project and still support the organization's goals. Project offices that want to appear responsive will respect the existing approaches, not arbitrarily declare them wrong or obsolete because they don't pass some new statistically derived muster.

A vendor selling me a software package recently argued against one of his competitors by saying the other software would lose credibility on setting duration "past the second decimal." I clarified that he meant point-00, and he said yes. As I walked away, I reflected on my concern for the profession. Project standardization and clarification of standards does not mean that we all have to adhere to second-decimal management. Most organizations would be thrilled if we could accurately predict cost or schedule to a whole number. Would a second-decimal prediction be more desirable? Sure. But will it lead to greater adherence? I think not. If we can expand the tool kit, and be open to broader application of the tools, we can show project management for what it is: an in-the-trenches practice in which we draw on the people, skills, and expertise available to make deliverables happen.

* * *

The Tao, The *I Ching,* and a Little Non-Western Project Management Attitude

Applying Eastern Philosophical Perspective in a Rigidly Western Practice

(March 2008)

Those of you who actually know me personally know that I am firmly rooted in my opinions, energized in my public demeanor, and unashamed of my fundamental role as "geek extraordinaire." Thus any discussion on those contemplative, meditative, and introspective practices of classic Eastern thought might seem out of place. But just as Richard Nixon was the right guy to go to China, I may be the right guy to bring a sense of equilibrium to the table for project management.

For those who have never done any homework in the *I Ching* (which translates to the *Book of Changes*) (Wilhelm and Baynes, 1967), it's often referred to as a fortune-telling device. Nothing could be further from the truth. It's actually a tool used to assess one's own attitudes in a context not previously been considered. In his study of the *I Ching,* titled *The Eleventh Wing* (Dheigh 1974), Khigh Dheigh examines that notion and strives to drive home the nature of the *Book of Changes.* (As a sidebar, those of you who have never read Khigh Dheigh might have seen him in the classic '70s police show *Hawaii 5-0,* as the insidious Wo Fat).

Carl, how does this relate to project management?

In project management, we are often called upon to take on the role of prognosticators, as well as the role of seers of our own environment. And we are asked to cope with change. What better place to start than with the ancient *Book of Changes*? (You can check out an online version at www.cfcl.com/ching/.) If you read a selection or two, you will find yourself wondering what the heck does that mean? The idea behind understanding it is to create your interpretation. That's the whole point. That's what the *Book of Changes* is largely about.

How does this relate to project management? Well, for one thing, project management is about nothing so much as about change. As you study the *I Ching*, you begin to understand that it thrives on a simple dichotomy of thought. There is what is. There is what isn't. And there is merit in both. Part of the thinking here is that it's important to pay homage and reverence to both sets of conditions. Even as we create something new, there is a need to explore and retain that of value from the old.

The *I Ching* is about personal interpretation. It's about taking what's been written, said, or done and making sure you have a deep grasp of what it means to you. It's not someone else's interpretation—it's yours. When you read in *A Guide to the Project Management Body of Knowledge* that risk management is designed (in part) to "increase the probability and impact of positive events," the question is what does that mean to you. Do you really have an interpretation for yourself that is meaningful? Could you defend that interpretation to someone else?

For some, it might simply mean that an objective of risk management is to create a sound business case. For others, it could mean that an objective of risk management is to create an environment in which the positive is more readily visible and attainable through the application of tools, metrics, and monitors. Is either perspective wrong? No. And in sifting through the available tool set, are there tools that I might find meaningful and you may not? Of course. But the key is to have a personal understanding. It is not enough to know words. What's important is to know what they mean to you and to still have enough mental bandwidth to know that there is merit in the alternative perspective—it's just not your perspective.

Western philosophy is often rooted in Calvinistic certitude. It is grounded in the notion that there are right and wrong answers, and our objective, personally and professionally, should be to discern and preach the right answers. The *I Ching* is grounded in the notion that there are multiple answers to every question, and they must be interpreted by the individual in a given situation, without being dismissive of the alternatives.

Although project management often seems to be a practice entrenched in the single right answer, we must take a somewhat Eastern philosophical moment to consider that the other answers have merit in their own context, application, and interpretation. If we can at least acknowledge their relative merit, we have the opportunity to open a healthier dialogue with our customers, team members, and professional peers.

* * *

PROCESS: CLOSING

SpongeBob SquarePants®, PMI®, and the Body of Project Ideas

Dealing with the Notion of Intellectual Property, Copyright, and Other Controlling Legal Concerns

(May 2003)

"A string walks into a bar..." My wife heard me telling that ancient joke the other day and reminded me, "Hey! That's my joke!"

"And you're proud of that?" I offered.

"No. But it's my joke. You're telling my joke." She shook her head. "You didn't even laugh when I told it to you." She paused. "And besides, it's my joke!"

I took further note the other night as I was framing a SpongeBob SquarePants poster. There he was. Friend to Squidward and all humanity. Nestled against a small, but noticeable, copyright symbol. According to that symbol, SpongeBob belongs to Viacom. Ask any young person, and they will inform you that SpongeBob belongs to the ages. (If you've been avoiding television for the past five years, SpongeBob is the bright yellow square of a cartoon character that rules a significant portion of the preteen market).

Read the *PMBOK® Guide* (Project Management Institute 2008) lately? It's teeming with copyright, service mark, and trademark notices. At least ten different copyright, service mark, and trademark notices are incorporated on the first page alone. But who owns the ideas?

The Power of a Copyright

Most people don't realize that when they craft something, and it represents a complete, new idea, it's copyrighted. No government intervention required. If you write an article, a story, or a letter and assert that it's yours and it's your original thought, it is copyrighted. Although you could submit the forms to formally copyright it through the government, even without its assistance, you legally have rights to your own ideas. The challenge comes in defending those rights. Whoever can make the best claim to ownership and can prove who was first with the idea, and that it's truly a unique, complete thought, will win.

The country music group the Dixie Chicks learned how little it takes to constitute a unique, complete thought when they used the phrase *I'll fly away* in their song "Sin Wagon." The original idea was Albert Brumley's from 1929. It's not public property until 2029. Those three little words, set to music, sent Brumley's heirs to take on Sony in the courts.

After the 9/11 tragedy, some charity groups tried to trademark the phrase *Let's roll*, as it was used on Flight 93 (the flight that crashed in Shanksville, Penn.). It was deemed too broadly used to be appropriate for trademark.

But how does this relate to project management? Projects are unique. As such, each project generates a new set of ideas, thoughts, and powerful approaches. Each project affords us the opportunity to build the base set of knowledge. With America's propensity for litigation, this opens the door for a whole new industry in the competition for ownership of ideas.

One organization that takes its copyrights, trademarks, and service marks seriously is the Project Management Institute. When authors agree to join in PMI projects, one of the institute's first acts is to get a signed agreement to clarify that PMI will become the sole owner of the content. The tight reins ensure that there's no lack of clarity about where the information is coming from (and conversely, when information is not coming from the institute).

The Power of Free Ideas

Does this mean that we should all follow PMI's example of ardently, passionately protecting each thought we share? No ... and yes. Free ideas provide project managers with the foundation for moving from project to project with a better base of information. Knowledge is power. But knowledge is power only when that knowledge is put to use or shared. The power of ideas produces something only when it is unleashed.

So how can we share ideas and information freely without losing our ownership? We mark it as our own. We provide it openly and freely but surround it with our own stamp. That stamp may take the shape of introductory notes about the use of a process (richly littered with the names of those who developed it), or it may simply be an assertion of copyright. PMI did this brilliantly in the 1996 edition of the *PMBOK®️ Guide,* with the copyright legend that read: "Permission to republish in full is granted freely." It meant that the document would remain whole and intact as they had intended, and yet the information could spread far more readily than would have otherwise been possible.

The liberal sharing of ideas with clear labels opens the door to spread the gospel of project management without surrendering pride of authorship and ownership. Will there be those who take credit for your ideas? Absolutely. But as long as you are keeping those ideas fresh, and building on them, you will remain one step ahead of the curve, and you have the advantage of knowing the thinking that established those ideas in the first place. You have the history. You know the groundwork and where it came from.

But ...

Not every idea can be shared with such liberality. Some

concepts, notions, and thoughts are intensely proprietary and owned by others. And many are covered by nondisclosure agreements (NDAs) or copyrights. If you encounter such a notion but wish there were a way to use it, don't. Don't accede to that temptation. If you're compelled to use something like it, then find an alternative source for the information before taking a single step forward.

There are sources for almost any information. The U.S. government has rich repositories of everything from photographs and art to articles and research. And, for the most part, if the government creates it, it is in the public domain. It may not be a mirror image of what you're looking for, but you might be able to find a process, procedure, or practice that meets the need. And then you know you're in the clear.

Ideas can be harnessed for only a short time. And they're new for only a short time. Sharing your thoughts liberally will ultimately get you credit for them. Ensuring other's ideas you share are legitimate and in the public domain will keep you out of trouble.

* * *

Project Management Theories of Relativity

Looking at How We Leverage Both Lessons Learned and Old Projects into New Ideas

(November 2003)

I just returned from a trip to England and Scotland and had the opportunity to do a bit of touring while I was there. I was continually stunned by the ancient nature of everything I saw. Edinburgh Castle, built in the 1100s, seemed virtually neolithic by American standards. St. Paul's Cathedral in

London was first established in 604 (and no, I didn't forget to put a *1* in front of it). By the time I went to the Stonehenge and Avebury stone circles, most of America's history seemed downright fresh.

What does this have to do with project management? Everything. Each site I visited had a history. Someone left it behind for the ages. These were projects on an epic scale. Stonehenge and Avebury took hundreds of years to complete. The walls within London Tower (actually well inside the gates of the Tower of London) are built in part on older Roman walls left behind in the second century. Although these ancient builders didn't leave behind their work breakdown structures, they did leave behind some lessons learned—lessons that are rooted in the sheer magnitude and epic nature of their history. And lessons affirm that in project management, everything's relative.

Don't just think of the first life cycle. A significant chunk of England is built on someone else's efforts. Stonehenge is now considered a natural treasure. Several hundred years ago, though, local farmers thought it a downright convenient collection of stones to help build their farmhouses. The joints in the stones and their construction made them ideal targets for reuse. As we build our projects, we may seriously wish to consider how others may look at them five and ten years down the road. That kind of future thinking can set the stage for a long-term respect for the longevity of that which we craft.

Your project is big, but someone else's may still be even more important. The etymology of the phrase *robbing Peter to pay Paul* may actually have its roots in project management. In 1540, St. Peter's in Westminster was upgraded from abbey church to cathedral. But when it was joined to the London diocese just ten years later (ahh, the joys of new management), many of its funds were appropriated for repairs on St. Paul's.

No matter how well you plan it, someone will misuse

it eventually. The stone circle of Avebury stretches a quarter of a mile across and is a marvel of ancient engineering. The stones weigh in excess of forty tons each and were put in place before Stonehenge was completed. In the excavation of the site, a discovery was made that was incongruous with other findings. It seems that although the stones were placed in ancient times, during England's medieval period, some poor fellow was playing on one of them, and it teetered over and crushed him like a grape. There are limits to how much you can "dummy proof" any system.

There's always one more way to fix it. As we walked through the Tower of London, the Beefeaters explained how the Roman walls became the tower walls and how the tower complex became the castle and how the Traitor's Gate became the access way and how the area over the gate became a chapel and so on and so on. In any project management effort, ours is not the last word. We learn new things. We see new possibilities. It's not always scope creep. In many instances, it's a function of opportunity rearing its lovely head.

What's the lesson learned in all this? We learn that all these things that we're experiencing as project managers are not new lessons. (The punishment for failure now may be termination, but in the 1500s and 1600s that had a completely different set of implications.) When we become frustrated with our management or customers and their propensity for change or their shifting perceptions on the projects, we should seriously consider that such changes in approach and attitude are nothing new. They've been around since truly ancient times and are often the forefathers of opportunity, rather than of pain and grief. Those ancient builders of Stonehenge had no idea they'd be making life much easier for English farmers millennia hence. The builders of the tower castle loo (restroom) in 1066 certainly couldn't have predicted the giggles they would evoke from children nearly a thousand years later.

We can take advantage of this in a number of ways. First, we can take comfort that someone, somewhere, some*when* will share our vision of the possibilities of projects we work on. Eventually, someone will appreciate our efforts. It doesn't do a lot for our current bosses, but it does afford some limited validation to our work.

Secondly, we can begin looking for the possibilities that our projects present before someone else does. Projects open up new possibilities. If we're the first to spot them, we may be the ones perceived as visionaries, but it takes a willingness to see what we're doing in a different light and to work out different perceptions of how and where our efforts may be applied.

Project management is relative. And from the ancient builders of Stonehenge to the team that erected the London Eye (the Millennium Ferris Wheel), it becomes a matter of getting others to not only share the vision of what the project is supposed to be but also to work toward what the project could become in the days, weeks, years—and beyond—to come.

* * *

Project Cabin Fever

As Projects Draw Near to Their Conclusion, We Need to Examine the Ongoing Motivation to See Them through to Fruition

(April 2004)

This year's winter seemed longer than many of recent memory. A few extra cloudy days, a few extra inches of snow, and the days seem to drag. For those in the northern reaches, the last vestiges of a hard winter lingered—tempting us with tastes of spring and then quickly dropping back into those bitter cold nights. What did most people want? Out. Just out. Just get me anywhere but here. The Caribbean would be nice. Southern California, perhaps? Hawaii? A day or two in the Congo even sounds alluring. The official answer? Anywhere but here.

Cabin fever is a common ailment, but it extends well beyond the limits of Mother Nature. Cabin fever extends to a lot of projects. *Cabin fever* is "the distress or anxiety caused by prolonged confinement in a small or remote place" (*The American Heritage Dictionary of Idioms*) (Ammer 2003). Projects are isolating events. By their very definition, they take us to the temporary universe of their specific goals. We don't get to work in the mainstream, basking in the sunshine of familiarity and common recognition. We work, instead, on the isolated crags of our unique endeavors. Here, because of the isolating nature of projects, we spend so much time that eventually the projects become a venue from which we crave an escape.

Example: You're working on a project that started last year and was supposed to be complete by October. Because of scope changes and modifications in approach and technology, it's still plodding along today, and the end may be months away. You had hoped that when it ended, you'd be able to catch up on some of those "other duties as assigned" that seem to keep falling by the wayside. The pile of other duties is mounting, and there's not a lot you can do about it. No one's complaining, but no one is quite clear on what you're working on. You can see the swelling volume of other work piling up around your desk.

The Nature of Cabin Fever

Think about what causes cabin fever. We don't get out. We don't interact with others. The familiar becomes contentious.

The sameness of the environment makes it unexciting, frustrating, and tiresome. At first, most people try to simply cope with the sameness, assuming it will end. Over time, however, its lingering nature builds upon itself to the point where the very consistency of the environment becomes the source of group angst.

Because of the repetitive nature of the situation, common solutions don't work. In some instances, the proposed solutions become sources of frustration in themselves. For example, you and your team have been having Friday meetings through the life of the project, as an opportunity for updates and a little camaraderie. They've largely degraded into whine fests with everyone wishing for an earlier end to the project. You dread them as much as any team member.

Beware! As spring approaches, the situation is going to get worse for project managers before it gets better. With real-world cabin fever coming to an end, folks will crave the opportunity to spend time outside, away from the office. They'll find the day-to-day grind of the cubicle even more confining rather than less.

Overcoming Cabin Fever

Get out, literally. One of the keys to dealing with cabin fever either in the real world or in our projects is to change the environment completely. Office space is inherently somewhat gray. Very few offices bear the bright sense of spring. They don't come across as cheery harbingers of better days ahead. But there are exceptions. One woman I used to work with always kept multiple flowers alive in her office and used them as décor in meeting rooms. It was a labor of love. And it changed the tone around her. Hers was an island of relief in an otherwise beige universe. Others have used posters, bright clothing. Others try food. One project manager in northern Virginia surprised a long-suffering team with a lobster bake in the conference room. Hold staff meetings in the open air.

But it's not all physical. It's mental, too. Give them a chance to try different tasks. Change approaches to your standard processes. Note that I didn't suggest that you change the process but change the way in which it's implemented. Take a different set of folks along on the next client site visit. Provide visibility and promote others by giving them roles in meetings, presentations, and project documentation. Trumpet small achievements.

One other approach doesn't involve changing the world around you. If all else fails, try what I found somewhat commonplace in late winter when I lived in Maine. When winter would stretch on into early April, my friends and I would celebrate the ongoing snow and cold. That's right, rather than curse the frustrations associated with one more day of gray slush at the side of the road, we'd celebrate. Acting like the latest round of snow was the first of the season, we'd invite friends over, make snowmen, and serve cocoa all around.

We can do that on our projects, renewing our sense of objectives, goals, and accomplishments. We can do it if we can genuinely immerse ourselves in the notion that by renewing it and cheering the environment in which we're working, we have the opportunity to bring ourselves closer to the end of the long winter of our project with a far better attitude.

❊ ❊ ❊

Giving the Gift of Change: The Twelve Lessons of Christmas

Using Lessons Learned from Our Personal Lives to Influence Our Project Universe

(December 2005)

Allow me a moment to delineate a few past gifts. Socks. A mechanical Uncle Sam bank. A tape recorder. A gift certificate. A collection of little metal brainteaser puzzles that remain unsolved. A T-shirt that reads "Is Anal Retentive Hyphenated?"

Each of these represents a different class of Christmas present. Things I didn't want but probably need. Things I didn't want but now cherish. Things I wanted. Things I have trouble remembering. Things that seemed neat at first but really just frustrate me now. And things I think show that others really understand me.

Those different classes of presents should have a familiar ring to project managers. They also sound eerily like change. We make changes all the time. There are constructive changes and changes that seem constructive but really just frustrate. There are changes that represent our vision and changes that represent the vision of our management (or the customer's management). There are changes made for change's sake and changes that truly enhance and enliven our lives' possibilities.

When looking at change, we can draw some powerful lessons from the stack of Christmas gifts received through the years. For the sake of this discussion, think of the client or customer as the recipient of the gift and the project organization as the giver.

Lesson 1: Know the environment in which the gift will be used. Giving a starving person a plastic snow globe represents the height of a lack of understanding. We need to know where the change will be used. If we understand the baseline culture and needs of the recipient, we won't make the mistake of implementing inappropriate changes.

Lesson 2: Know the recipient's approach to life/business well. A friend of ours recently gave a holiday gift of cash to another friend in need to help cover the mortgage. The giver, very prudently, withheld his name from the recipient. Why? The recipient would never have accepted that much cash from a friend. She willingly accepted it, however, from a "secret Santa." The donor knew who would be dealing with the change and under what conditions the change would be acceptable.

Lesson 3: Give in reasonable doses. Change may be welcome. But in volume, it can be downright damaging. Ever get a mountain of presents as an adult? It can be almost embarrassing. At best, it's overwhelming. My wife found an interesting way to solve this. It was an advent "program of giving" for her sister. She got her sister a gift a day for the advent season. The myriad small gifts piled up and opened at once would have been almost onerous. Given over the weeks of Advent, it became a positive adventure. If we must implement a host of changes, we should think through how we can program them to suit the customer's calendar and timing.

Lesson 4: Give freely. If you've ever participated in a gift exchange where some of the participants were unwilling, it was downright awkward (and perhaps even painful). Yes, they offered presents. But they may as well have been offering dental exams. Similarly, with changes, we will have to implement them. They are a necessity of project management. However, the attitude goes a long way toward determining whether we're perceived as supporters of the change or merely along for the ride in the client experience.

Lesson 5: Know your limits and theirs. There's nothing

worse than giving a fruitcake to someone who in turn gives you a Rolex watch. If the client has a $20,000 budget, be careful not to recommend a $100,000 change.

Lesson 6: Make it personal. Change is not a personal experience. But it represents personal stakes and personal interests. Because the client asked for the change, we should strive to make it look, act, feel, smell, or be the way it was envisioned. And assuming it's a constructive change, don't be afraid to trumpet it as [trumpet fanfare here] "(Customer's Name)'s Change!"

Lesson 7: Make it usable. Some gifts require coaching. If you gave my wife's grandfather a high-end computing workstation, he might use it to produce a document or two. But ask him to edit and burn a few DVDs, and he'd be out of his league. When we offer changes, we need to make sure that the recipient is ready for them, knows how to apply them, and understands the nature of the beast. If not, we may take what was a perfectly acceptable environment and rework it to be annoying and unusable.

Lesson 8: Reassess the environment. Earlier, I stressed the need to look at the environment for your change. If you haven't done so lately, do it again. Every year, we bought my father-in-law tools for the holidays. In the past two years, his eyesight has begun to fail. It leads to a completely different tack for gift giving. The client is the same, the wants and needs are much the same, but the environment has changed. Now, virtually all gifts are channeled to meet a new set of needs. We need to be sure we're looking at the client we have today and not the one we had several years ago.

Lesson 9: Incorporate those whom you support. Gift giving and change both often rely on outsiders. Salespeople, subcontractors, vendors, and delivery personnel all get involved in the process. Sometimes, in the haste of the season (of change), we forget who our best supporters have been on the other side. Change is a wonderful opportunity to optimize our use of those we support most. They should be the first line of consideration when the need arises to support new needs.

Lesson 10: Offer alternatives. Finding gifts for those who have it all is sometimes the greatest challenge for holiday shoppers. What about the clients who really don't need change? Maybe we can help them find the perfect surprise for themselves. Help them identify different options and some improvements. Give them the opportunity to try something completely different. The trick is to explore the possibilities with the client first before you decide on the perfect option.

Lesson 11: Consider the time/timing. This year, I received one of the most clever Christmas cards ever. And it wasn't even a Christmas card. It was a Thanksgiving card. In an effort to beat the rush and stand alone, a professional peer sent out Thanksgiving cards. Think of all the implications. There's no risk of being politically incorrect. There's no chance of being lost in a sea of Christmas cards. There's no chance of offending those who celebrate Hanukkah or Kwanzaa. And, there was time to really read what was written on the card. It was sheer brilliance. The ordinary was rendered extraordinary by timing alone. Similarly, when we accept changes, how we stage the timing of the changes and our ability to meet the planned time can make all the difference in the world in building positive relationships.

Lesson 12: Make it consistent with expectations. I got a $12,000 bonus! Oh, gosh, I got the Jelly-of-the-Month Club. There's the ultimate embarrassing moment. How horrible is that! You gave one child the ultimate toy and the other a dozen pairs of socks. There's a simple way to avoid that. Be consistent. If we handle all our recipients with a reasonable level of equity and equanimity, we put ourselves in a position in which we won't feel compelled to explain away how and why we do what we do. With change control, it's much the same story. Stick to the program and make it consistent. It makes life a whole lot easier to track.

Will following these rules guarantee a better outcome for any gifts we might give? No. There are no guarantees. But will these ensure we're doing what we can to affirm that the changes that come our way are more likely to be deployed well and with cheer? Absolutely. These are ways to ensure that we build better relationships and have a better understanding of the directions those relationships are taking. And they open the door to examine change in a different light. Instead of perceiving it as a challenge, an onus, or a challenge to the customer relationship, we can begin to see change as a gift to be welcomed and given freely.

* * *

Celebrating the Inconsequential?

Drawing on Personal Experience to Find Reasons to Rebuild and Renew Project Energy through the Small Stuff

(October 2007)

This month, I turned fifty. The big five-oh. Time for the midlife crisis car (no fling required, as my wife is a goddess to be worshipped), major life reviews, and (my favorite part) chocolate cake! More than 18,000 days. More than 435,000 hours. More than 2.6 million minutes. Whew. That's a lot of time. But even so, a fiftieth birthday is just another day on the calendar. Should we really celebrate a mere flip of the calendar or click of the clock?

Allow me to be the first to offer a resounding yes!

Now it's not just because I'm the one hitting fifty. I actually got the idea for this article in a class I was teaching today. A woman in one of my classes, Christine, was having a birthday, and one of her co-workers got a cake and asked if I would be willing to pause for ten minutes for the celebration. Christine did not have your typical adult reaction to the surprise. When we announced the break, her reply was, "Great! I love this. I love birthdays. This is so nice. I can't tell you how much I appreciate it. Thanks!" Her response was warm and genuine. It was unequivocal. She was truly appreciative that those people in the room were joining her in acknowledging her special day.

As adults, we sometimes feign indifference by saying that such events are not necessary or too much bother. I think Christine's reaction was perfect. It was not too much bother. It was necessary. Not only was she excited about her birthday but she also wanted others to be there.

In the middle of a project, progress is often slow, if not downright glacial. It's moving, but it's very hard to see the motion. In many cases, we soldier on, pushing ahead with our work but not feeling the satisfaction we somehow sense that we should. And if someone does acknowledge our accomplishments, we feel somehow tainted if we don't downplay it with comments like "just doing my job", or "no problem". We should take a lesson from Christine, genuinely celebrating the opportunities that the situation affords. Even more, we should take a page from Christine's co-worker, who so adroitly acknowledged a day that would have passed like any other, but instead became a special team moment.

The passage of time is amazing. My wife's grandfather is in his mid-90s and remarkably sharp. Every day of his life is now a treasure. My wife and I are nearing our twenty-fourth anniversary. Having put up with me for that length of time, she deserves acknowledgement. A peer's project is now entering its third year (when it was supposed to be done in two). Is that a cause for celebration? In my mind, it definitely should be. We need to revel in the fact that the organization still sees it as sufficiently valuable to warrant ongoing investment. We need to rejoice that the customer is still anxiously awaiting the deliverables. We need to provide a pat on the back to those team members who have been with the project for an extended period and remain dedicated to its completion.

Carl, isn't that just damning with faint praise? Don't we run the risk of creating a sense that we'll acknowledge things that really aren't worth acknowledging, or worse? Don't we run the risk of encouraging projects to drag out?

I won't say those aren't risks. But I think they're outweighed by the authentic and very personal need of each human being for a modicum of recognition. We all need some basic appreciation that we are contributing members of our respective communities, and we need the nod that our contributions are not altogether ordinary. In some instances, that sense of the extraordinary need be no more than a round of applause or a meeting acknowledgement or a small cake shared amongst peers. If it is offered with a true sense of appreciation for contributions, achievement, or even just the significant passage of time, we open the door for the Christine-like gratitude of those who are willing to accept and embrace it. If we fall short on such acknowledgements, those team members who do need them will be left wanting unnecessarily.

✳ ✳ ✳

Professional Responsibility

Where Do We Go from Here?
More Than 330,000 PMPs and Climbing

A Glimpse into the Crystal Ball of Professionalism

(May 2001, updated 2009)

As an industry, despite the economic sluggishness, project management is still rolling through a boom cycle. The Project Management Institute boasts that more than 330,000 of us have overcome the hurdles to become certified as Project Management Professionals. That's a huge number, 330,000, compared to a couple of decades ago. I should know. That's when I got my certification. Certificate 1049. Back then, the problem was not about how to continue to energize and grow the profession, but instead just how to get people to stop mispronouncing the PMP acronym.

For the most part, we are past those hurdles. The profession is recognized, at least to the point where most of us are not spending a significant portion of our lives trying to identify what it is we do for a living. The challenge now is to take project management to the next level. Different organizations are taking different tactics, and that's fine. Some are pushing project management offices. Others are striving to find new types of certifications to ensure that everyone is meeting personal development needs. Still others are generating methodologies, templates, and historical repositories where none existed before. These are all powerful and exciting trends. They have the potential to keep project management in the fore for a long time to come.

Still, there are valuable historical lessons to be

learned from past business practices. Perhaps the most instructive is the quality movement. Quality went from being a simple catchphrase to becoming a guiding force in international business in the course of a mere thirty years. Project management is in the midst of a similar business transformation cycle. Quality continues to be a driving force, but not in the way it once was. Quality circles and Total Quality Management (TQM) are sometimes the subjects of derision. Not because they have no value, but because they have become almost a cliché in their business application. That's a key lesson learned here. Don't let the terms define the profession. Instead, we should embrace the diversity of project management practice. Nothing makes this point more powerfully than a simple list of the sometimes competing, sometimes complementary support structures for project management. If you ever want a lesson in how else to do it, consider some of these documents as references:

- ISO 10006: the project management quality guideline (International Organization for Standardization 2003)

- *PMBOK® Guide*, 4th edition: the latest iteration of PMI's *A Guide to the Project Management Body of Knowledge*

- *PMBOK® Guide*, 3rd edition: the standard under which PMI saw its largest period of growth

- *PMBOK® Guide*, 1996: the outdated version

- *PMBOK® Guide*, 1987: a dated, but powerful standard

- *APM Body of Knowledge*: the Association for Project Management's version of all you need to know (Association for Project Management 2006)

- *British Standard 6079–4*: prepared under the direction of the British Management Systems Sectors Board (British Standards Institution 2006)

- *Australian Standard for Risk Management (AS/NZS 4360)*: a risk-specific project management standard (Standards Australia 2004)

And there are many others. The key is not to consistently invent new practices for project management, but instead to learn the existing practices well. It's a safe bet that most project managers have never seen at least two of the documents listed in the preceding paragraph. And they offer new perspectives and insights (despite their age) worthy of serious consideration. If we're looking for somewhere to go as a profession, let's work toward knowing the body of existing information, knowledge, and practice rather than striving to find new ways to slice the same orange.

If we want to grow, let's grow from the existing knowledge base, and there's plenty of it out there.

* * *

PMP, EVP, CPA, M-O-U-S-E

Sure, You're Certified, But Is It the Right Certification?

(May 2005, updated 2009)

My wife, Nancy, is a CPA (certified public accountant). When she sat for the exam at the Maryland State Fairgrounds in Timonium, there were just slightly more than 1,000 test takers. Of that group, forty earned their certification that day. Forty. That's 4 percent; 4 percent of those who sat for the exam earned the right to put CPA after their name. The pass rate on the PMP (Project Management Professional) project management certification exam is reported at between 60 and 70 percent. The Pennsylvania State Bar exam had a 2004 pass rate of about 80 percent. Does this say it's tougher to be a CPA than a PMP? And tougher to be a PMP than a lawyer? Not necessarily.

What it does say is there are hurdles to be overcome to be recognized as skilled professionals. But the question becomes one of which skills are we emphasizing. In 1992, there were fewer than 1,000 PMP-certified project managers. Today, the count is more than 330,000. In June 2005, the (AACE) Association for the Advancement of Cost Engineering International rolled out the (EVP) Earned Value Professional certification exam (www.aacei.org). It was piloted in New Orleans. It went nationwide the following July. (ASAPM) the American Society for the Advancement of Project Management (www.asapm.org) plans to roll out a competency-based certification as part of its 2005 agenda. Certifications abound. IPMA (the International Project Management Association) has a competency-based certification model. More options, both general and specific, are cropping up. The key is going to be to recognize which are valid and requisite to be acknowledged as a professional certification and which are just initials that roll out after your name.

Picking a Certification

To put the current quandary in perspective, the first public accounting societies formed in the late 1880s. Despite efforts at cooperation and early certification, the CPA in its modern form really didn't take hold until the mid-1930s. That's fifty years without certainty as to how the certification would shape up.

The past decade has seen a proliferation of certifications. From software certifications to the exponential growth of the PMP, more and more organizations are looking to certify their members as competent professionals. But a valuable lesson may be learned from our friends, the accountants. According to the *Journal of Accountancy* (Previts 1996), the 1936 merger of the largest accounting associations paved the way for true professionalism in accounting. It then opened doors as it created an environment in which true standards could be established, audited, and enforced.

Today, by contrast, different professional associations of every stripe strive to generate interest and support for various certification programs. Consider the list of certifications that a rudimentary Google search generates:

- BJCP (Beer Judge Certification Program)

- ESTCP (Environmental Security Technology Certification Program)

- CSDP (Certified Software Development Professional)

- LPIC (Linux Professional Institute Certification)

- CFCM (Certified Federal Contracts Manager)

- CCCM (Certified Commercial Contracts Manager)

- CPCM (Certified Professional Contracts Manager)

- Certified MBTI (Myers–Briggs Type Indicator) Professional

And the list goes on. In fact, a search for *.org* with the term *certification program* yields just under a million hits.

Picking the right one has its rewards. Project managers who got in on PMP certification early take great pride in having PMP registration numbers under 100 (or even fewer than 1,000). That's why it's noteworthy that two new certifications made their debut that summer. With ASAPM and AACE both adding fuel to the certification fire, the question is whether the certifications will last. If they do, early participation has its rewards. To be among the early adopters later in a career makes one seem more sage, more insightful, and more grounded in the profession. However, if the certifications don't have staying power, it can be an exercise in administrative procedure with little or no reward.

Testing for Certification Staying Power

How do you know? First, look at who's behind it. The individuals in charge should be recognized, published players in the field. Do they have the credentials and the broad national (or international) support to make it work? ASAPM has the big plus of being allied with IPMA. AACE has a historic working relationship with PMI. Do they have the membership to make it happen? IPMA's reach is extensive in Europe and Asia. The organization may have the potential for influence on ASAPM's behalf. AACE has its tendrils woven deep in the federal government community, and with those alliances, it may have potential. AACE has been around for half a century.

Is the certification for real? Is there a challenge associated with getting it? Does it require more than just a rubber stamp and a check? Assuming so, that's a key component. If it's too easy to achieve, its weight will rapidly vanish.

Will the certification last? That's a question sometimes tied to how long the profession will last. Although still recognized as an achievement, the ICCP (Institute for Certification of Computing Professionals) no longer lists the CDP (Certified Data Processor) as one of its active certifications. Although the credential is still worthwhile enough to be maintained on quite a few résumé, it's becoming a professional anachronism. The more narrow the certification, the greater the possibility it may be supplanted by a newer approach or technology. Still, the narrower the certification, the more powerful the acknowledgement that you are its master.

Where Do We Go from Here?
For those of us who are already certified, the next question is whether to go down another certification path or take another step forward. My contention is yes. There's value in the rigors of any certification process, even if the value doesn't come from the letters one gets to pin after his name. The value comes from the forced march through a new set of content, the drive to clarify the nuances of a practice, and the satisfaction of knowing that the old dog can learn new tricks. The value also comes from being able to cite oneself as a ready adopter to new approaches to information and new ways of doing business or as a veteran who truly understands the intricacies of the old ways.

* * *

LIGHTER FARE

A Holiday Parody

With Apologies to a Certain Mr. Moore

(December 2000)

'Twas the night before D–Day and the project was due.
All the team members, customers, stakeholders knew.
The plans were established, all signed off with care
In hopes that deliverables soon would be there.
The team members hammered away at their work
While visions of comp time hung out as a perk.
And the team in their cubes and me at my station
Had just settled in for the last-ditch gyrations.
When over the phone there arose such a clatter
The customer wanted to know what was the matter;
Away to the e-mail I flew like a flash,
Threw open my Outlook, and sifted through trash.
When what to my wondering eyes should appear
But a massive new change order, details unclear,
With a little old change clause just written so well—
I knew in a moment the other shoe fell.
They knew it would have to be done—they're no fools
So I called for the whole pile of management tools:
"A Gantt Chart, A PERT Chart, A network, a plan!
A GERT Chart, Pareto, Decision Trees, man!"
To the conference room, to the customer call
Now plan away, plan away, plan away all.
To the Post-its and scratch pads the team members flew
With heads full of plans and alternatives, too.

And then from my team member I heard one great thought
"Make sure the customer can see what they've bought!"
As I pondered the statement and turned it around,
The customer entered the room with a bound.
She was dressed in her business suit, looking concerned,
"My game plan has changed, our approaches have turned!"
A bundle of problems she poured on the table
And babbled in technospeak's tower of Babel.
She needed more GUI! She needed some data!
She needed e-commerce! She needs it pro rata!
Her eyes how they darted! Her brow how it furrowed!
Her hands how they sweat as through papers she burrowed.
She had a clear mission, at least in her mind,
But in sharing her vision, she was leaving us blind.
We shared a few words, and then went straight to our work;
She wasn't confused, or a pain, or a jerk,
But taking some time and just talking it through,
Some clarity finally began to brew.
She opened her eyes and she thanked us profusely
For firming up statements she had stated so loosely.
And I heard her exclaim as she strolled down the hall—
"Merry Projects to You! Merry Projects to All!"

* * *

A Visit from the Project Manager: 'Twas the Night before the PMP Exam

With Still More Apologies to Clement Clark Moore

(November 2002)

'Twas the night before testing,
And all through the team
Not a member was stirring—nor working—it seemed.
The prep work was done by the students with care,
In hopes that their efforts some fruit it would bear.
The hopefuls were nestled all snug in their beds,
While visions of PMPs danced in their heads;
And PMBOKs in storage, and quiz books at rest,
We all settled in for one night 'fore the test.
When out of my pocket I heard that loud beep,
I fished for my cell phone that ruined my sleep.
I grabbed for my glasses and reached for my slacks,
And prayed for some life left in battery packs.
The moon on the breast of the new-fallen snow
Meant some risk event caused by delays, don't you
    know.
When, what to my wondering eyes should appear,
But a man with a Gantt chart, and books piled up to
    here.
Yes, that little old project manager, so lively was he,
I knew in a heartbeat, it was Sir PMP.
More jargon than techies he had at his hand,
And the authors of project-stuff at his command.
"Now, Kerzner! now, Cleland! now, Verma and Fleming!
On, Meredith! Mantel! on, Ward, Frame, and Deming!
To the PDM chart! to the WBS!
Now analyze! Quantify! Estimate! Guess!"
As tough bosses can make the wild estimates fly,

So on the exam make your best guess, just try,
So on to Prometrics the testers they flew,
With their heads full of data, and their ID cards, too.
And then, in four hours, from the test centers came
The moaning and praying of testers in pain.
I clipped on my cell phone, was turning around,
The first scores of PMPs came out with a bound.
They were bathed in a glow, from their plan to their charter,
They all seemed much brighter, much better, much smarter.
A command of the tools from the PMBOK® had they
And a sense of the processes—Z back to A.
Their scores—how they tallied! They *passed!* It was heaven—
And they didn't mind it was by 137.
Their coats now had pins just above the lapel,
The PMP logo was there for to tell
They endured the challenge, and bore the good news,
Their lives now revolved around more PDUs.
The credential they wore like a warrior's medal,
Their project they knew now would be in fine fettle.
Sir PMP nodded, so proud of his students.
He knew they'd stick to their professional prudence,
He knew that they'd dig in and make this all work,
WBS and Gantt and earned value and PERT.
He rolled up his risk plan and he praised the new passers,
"You folks are the best, all the new project masters."
And I heard him exclaim, 'ere his plan was delayed,
"Happy Christmas to All, You Have All Made the Grade."

* * *

A Baker's Dozen of Holiday Classics and the Project Management Lessons They Teach

A Look at How the Lessons of Our Movie Classics Tie Directly to the Profession

(December 2003)

Home Alone

The story of a team member left completely to his own devices, with no supervision, succeeding in the face of adversity.

Lessons learned: Stock the team refrigerator well. Provide direction. Tell the neighboring project managers to keep an eye on things.

A Charlie Brown Christmas

The story of a self-managed work team putting on a major production with no visible management support.

Lessons learned: One team's dead twig is another's mighty fir. Don't discount the potential of team members who buy into a vision.

Holiday Inn

The tale of one nefarious project manager scheming for the opportunity to get the resources of an honest, well-meaning project manager.

Lessons learned: The good guys ultimately win, if they sometimes resort to the bad guy's tactics.

How the Grinch Stole Christmas

Another tale of unauthorized resource appropriation.

Lessons learned: Sooner or later, the resources have to go back to Whoville. And sooner or later, the team members (Max) need a chance to ride, instead of pull, the sleigh.

A Christmas Story

The story of a customer (Ralphie) who believes that wants have become needs.

Lessons learned: If the customer believes it, sooner or later management believes it.

The Santa Clause

The story of a man converted by a change in objective, direction, and vision.

Lessons learned: Rapidly graying hair and an extra forty pounds may accompany radical changes in direction. Learn to laugh about it.

Rudolph the Red-Nosed Reindeer

A jolly old project manager with high risks and short-term deliverables enlists unlikely resources in getting his project (and his sleigh) off the ground.

Lessons learned: Even the resources who don't fit the organization's mold (yes, even Yukon Cornelius) can bring something to the table. Also, allow time for reindeer games.

Miracle on 34th Street

Another jolly old project manager finally gets formal authority, thanks to a court battle and the U.S. Postal Service.

Lessons learned: Authority is sometimes a function of sheer numbers of believers. Get enough people behind you, and they'll believe you *are* the project manager.

Christmas Vacation

A diligent team member is insulted by his corporate reward: the jelly-of-the-month-club.

Lessons learned: If you're a performer, work is its own reward. You'll get a lot more satisfaction out of throwing the switch on your own display than you will waiting for management to appreciate you.

Frosty the Snowman

A visiting consultant vaporizes as a project heats up, vowing to return in more temperate times.

Lessons learned: There is no magic hat. Consultants function because we believe in what they're doing.

White Christmas

A major project is taken from New York and brought to the remote mountains of Vermont, where it restores hope to a man and an organization that disbanded years earlier.

Lessons learned: Some projects aren't about the money, but you still need to let management know when costs will exceed "ouch" or "wow."

It's a Wonderful Life

A team member loses $8,000 to an unscrupulous customer, putting his manager in jeopardy. Every ally rallies round the manager to save him from prosecution and jail time.

Lessons learned: Quoting from the movie, "No man is a failure who has friends." (And it doesn't hurt if they have a little cash. Hee-haw!)

Dick Clark's Rockin' New Year's Eve

Hundreds of thousands gather to watch the last ten seconds of a major project, televised to millions around the planet.

Lessons learned: If you're going to drop the ball, do it in style.

Happy holidays!

* * *

The Folks of Summer: Casey, the Project Manager

With Apologies to Ernest L. Thayer

(August 2004)

As the summer winds down, it seems only appropriate to pay homage to the boys of summer in a project context (Thayer 1912).

Casey at the Schmooze

The outlook wasn't brilliant for the project team that day,

The customer was whining, and they weren't going to pay.

And then when Einstein left the project, and Beavis did the same,

A pall-like silence fell upon the workers who remained.

A straggling few got transferred out in deep despair. The rest

Clung to that hope which springs eternal in the human breast.

They thought, "If only Casey could but share with them the news.

We'd put up even money now, with Casey at the schmooze."

But meetings hindered Casey, as did also coffee breaks;

And the former went for hours, while no progress they did make.

So upon that stricken project team, grim melancholy oozed,

For there seemed but little chance of Casey getting to the schmooze.

But the meeting actually ended, to the wonderment of all.

And the coffee break was short, and Casey made it down
the hall.
And when the dust had lifted, and they saw what had
occurred,
There was Casey with the customer and Einstein's voice
was heard.
Then from the project team and boss there rose a lusty
yell;
It rumbled through the valley, it rattled in the dell;
It pounded through on the mountain and recoiled with
a rant;
For Casey, mighty Casey, showed the customer the
Gantt.
There was ease in Casey's manner as he stepped into his
place,
There was pride in Casey's bearing and a smile lit Casey's
face.
And when, responding to the questions, he nodded to
the PERT,
No stranger on the team could doubt 'twas Casey on
alert.
Two dozen eyes were on him as he turned his slide show
on.
The voices all applauded with their fear of failure gone.
Then, while the one tough customer raised questions off
the hip,
Defiance flashed in Casey's eye, a sneer curled Casey's
lip.
A question on the due date came hurtling through the
air,
And Casey said, "We'll make the day," in haughty grandeur
there.
Close by the project manager, his VP, he did lean.
"I'm worried 'bout these milestones and deliverables
unseen."

From the cubicles and telecon, there was a muffled
    cough,
From the disbelieving doubters who all knew the VP's
    off.
"Stop him! Stop the management!" someone whispered
    in the band,
And it's likely they'd have killed him had not Casey raised
    his hand.
With a smile of Christian charity, great Casey's visage
    shone,
He stilled the rising tumult, as he led the meeting on.
He signaled to the customer to raise the next concern,
And they spoke of angry users and the help desk's failed
    returns.
The VP looked more worried as the customer outlined
Problem after problem, and the project firm maligned.
They talked of early closeout and of shutting things all
    down,
They talked of early settlement; said the PM was a
    clown.
The team saw Casey's face grow cold, they saw his temples
    strain,
And they knew that Casey wouldn't send the project
    down the drain.
The sneer has fled from Casey's lip, the teeth are clenched
    in rage.
He pulls the spec and project files, he flips from page to
    page.
A contract clause is cited, and vendor names are called,
And one last schmooze attempts to stop the cruelest blow
    of all.
Oh, somewhere in this favored land the sun is shining
    bright.
The band is playing somewhere, and somewhere hearts
    are light.

And, somewhere men are laughing, and managers all
  shout,
But there is no joy in Projectland—
Mighty Casey has struck out.

* * *

War of the Worlds: Lessons Learned
from the Martian Invasion

A Martian Project Manager's Perspective

(October 2006)

Project: Invasion of Earth
  Desired outcome: Colonization of New Mars
  Schedule: 120 years
  Actual outcome: Mission on hold after Phase II, under
reconsideration

What Went Right?

The team had an outstanding beginning and some of the
best minds on Mars came up with strategies to ensure that we
would have global infiltration and an effective means of craft
and personnel delivery. Suggested elements to keep from the
initiation processes:

Kickoff meeting: The kickoff meeting united the political
and logistical sides of the house by clearly defining the vision
and the approach. Without clarity on that, we probably
wouldn't have been able to get management to drag its
tentacles out of the Dark Ages and sign off on the thing.
Management's mark on the New Mars Pact was probably the
single most important thing we achieved.

Initial risk analysis: This will also show up under the
larger failings of the project, but it is noteworthy that we

did identify the risk that ultimately caused the project to be less of a success than it might otherwise have been. We identified risks very well in the attached document. Note that habitability was identified early on as a critical risk (granted it was also identified on the Mercury and Venus options). We tried to keep it upbeat and on an opportunity perspective by flagging planets as having the risk of being inhabitable rather than uninhabitable. In the future, a negative or threat perspective might be more appropriate in getting management to be sufficiently paranoid about the possibilities. Still, we take some silent pride in the fact that we did identify this from the very outset as one of the significant risks on the project. In retrospect, as is discussed later in this document, we might have wanted to actually do something with the risk document besides file it with management and load it into the New Home directory on the LAN.

Prototype pilot: Sending out an early mission was an act of sheer genius. It worked on a variety of levels. Who would have thought that the first canister would actually land in that movie director's estate? Mr. Spielberg took in one of our pilots, nursed him back to health, and sent him back to us. I understand that he later used elements of the visitation in a film. Unfortunately, when the pilot died upon his return to Mars, we presumed it was from Reese's Pieces poisoning. We posted alerts and warnings for all pilots to avoid these small comestibles but never imagined that something else also might have caused the pilot's illness. The mission (and subsequent film) did serve to create a sense of friendly aliens on Earth, something that worked very heavily to our advantage in the early hours of the invasion.

Launch timing: Our research into human behavior around holidays was invaluable. Launching the mission at Halloween (a human holiday involving bizarre costumes, excessive sugar intake, and vegetable defacement) was a masterstroke. It helped mask our true intent for hours, if not days. For the next assault (if we try again), we may wish to consider an attack nearer to the Winter Solstice, and dress our pilots in red uniforms with white trim. For some reason, humans consider individuals dressed in such a fashion to be their friends.

What Went Wrong?

Risk follow-through: Perhaps the greatest failing of the mission was that we never revisited the risk list that we generated in the early days of the project. In fact, we were so thrilled with our efforts up through the construction phase that very few of the actual flight and invasion risks were ever captured or dealt with. For future missions, we definitely need to revisit the risks at regular intervals. And we need to seriously exam those risks that involve total loss of mission crews. Management felt it was not sufficiently alerted to these, and that contention was backed up in the Greenmen Accountability Office (GAO) report that cited our risk efforts as deficient after the initial analysis. *Suggestion:* We should have gotten signatures from the head office on any risks that might have taken that heavy a toll.

Temporal and physical distance: Although there's nothing we could have done to lessen the temporal and physical distance between Mars and Earth, we should have taken into account that a team completely cut off from the home world would be in dire peril at some point. If it had not been a bacterial infection, some other Earthborne challenge may have invariably taken its toll on our personnel. *Suggestion:* We should have had regular rotations of personnel back from Earth and should have had a strategy for quick returns (a way station on the moon, perhaps?) that would not require that they bridge the entire gulf between the two planets.

Current Status

Management has indicated that the Earth Colonization

Project is on the back burner for the time being and may be seriously reconsidered in about two Earth decades. We strongly suggest that these lessons learned be made part of the project methodology before such an effort is undertaken. We also suggest that rather than dragging out the New Mars Project for another twenty years, this project be terminated and a new project be initiated when the organizational climate is more favorable. The taint of the existing project may linger for years to come, and there is no reason to saddle another project manager with the baggage from the original effort.

* * *

A Business Justification for Christmas by Ebenezer Scrooge, Project Manager

God Bless Us, Every One

(October 2006)

1.0 Executive Overview

Following an executive-level conference with former partner Jacob Marley, it is the considered opinion of this project manager that the holiday season, replete with all its trappings, is in the best interests of the organization and creates ample opportunities for us to not only celebrate our lives and our families but also increase the efficiency, productivity, and efficacy of our organization as a whole.

2.0 Project Description

Create or affirm an annual celebration marked by intense religious fervor, family renewal, and commercial investment on a scale unseen at other times of the year.

2.1 Proponent(s)

Supporters of this effort include not only members of the business community but also followers of religious movements, children, school administrators, football fanatics, grocers, pine tree growers, toy manufacturers, and those who pursue opportunities for self-examination and reflection.

2.2 Sponsor(s)

Sponsors include leaders of religious movements, business leaders, and the media. For many, there is only one sponsor of Christmas, and any other perceived sponsors are latecomers (by about 2,000 years) to the event.

2.3 Users/Beneficiaries

Children, people of faith, workers, the poor and destitute, and a world community of those who seek opportunities for celebration, joy, and outdoor decorating. In short, humankind.

2.4 Deliverables and Quality Criteria

Project will be considered complete (for this year) on Epiphany (twelve days after December 25) and when well-wishing (tangible and intangible) has been exchanged across parties, supplemental vacation time has been granted (and received), offices have been shuttered (albeit briefly), and team members have had the opportunity to share time and good spirit with each other. Exceptional quality has been achieved when the spirit of the season continues through the year.

2.5 Rationale

The project is borne out of the sage counsel of three spectral consultants who visited December 24. While acknowledging the financial success of our business, they were quick to highlight deficiencies of the organization in terms of support for and from the local community and in terms of acceptance of social responsibility.

2.6 Cost Benefit

Fred Holywell (a relative working in another line of business) put the financial case in somewhat idealistic terms when he said, "And therefore, uncle, though it has never put a scrap of gold or silver in my pocket, I believe that it *has* done me good, and *will* do me good; and I say, God bless it!" Although that perspective captures the idealistic perspective on the holiday, it does not capture the true cost-benefit.

If one examines the overall costs of the holiday, they include time granted to allow staff to spend both with family and with their employer (over a smoking bowl of Christmas bishop, as it were), as well as the lost work hours. However, the benefits reaped from a generous holiday package include the elimination of time spent grousing over employees feeling ill used because they didn't get the same level of performance support from their management and the sense of increased performance, motivation, and productivity resulting from their sense of being valued by the organization.

3.0 Strategic Alignment

3.1 Objectives Served

The following corporate objectives are served well by a generous implementation of holiday activity:

3.1.1 Corporate productivity is increased (on a per-working-day basis)

3.1.2 Revenue is enhanced (through more local support of Scrooge & Marley)

3.1.3 Customer base is increased (see above)

3.2 Portfolio Ranking

The project moves to the No. 1 position by virtue of the time of year. Given the schedule considerations, no other project should even be under serious consideration at this time.

4.0 Alternatives

4.1 Alternative Considered

The organization (for most of its history) has employed a strategy of devoutly ignoring the festivities. Last year's recommendations included treating those who observe the season by boiling them with their own pudding and burying them with a stake of holly through their respective hearts.

4.2 Rationale for Dismissal

The alternative was dismissed not only for the obvious legal implications, but also at the urging of the consultants mentioned earlier in this document.

5.0 Assumptions

We, as an organization, are striving to keep Christmas well, if any alive possess the knowledge. May that be truly said of us, and all of us!

6.0 Conclusion

Although the business justification is less than pure, I refer again to my nephew, Fred Holywell, for his gifted prose.

There are many things from which I might have derived good, by which I have not profited, I dare say, Christmas among the rest. But I am sure I have always thought of Christmas time, when it has come round—apart from the veneration due to its sacred name and origin, if anything belonging to it can be apart from that—as a good time; a kind, forgiving, charitable, pleasant time; the only time I know of, in the long calendar of the year, when men and women seem by one consent to open their shut-up hearts freely, and to think of people below them as if they really were fellow passengers to the grave, and not another race of creatures bound on other journeys. And therefore, uncle, though it has never put a scrap of gold or silver in my pocket, I believe that it has done me good, and will do me good; and I say, God bless it!

—Charles Dickens,
A Christmas Carol, Stave One (Dickens 1843)

* * *

The Blackberry Maven

With Apologies to Edgar Allan Poe

(October 2008)

Once upon a project dreary, at a meeting getting weary,
Over many a rehashed mound of data by a crashing bore,
Came a beeping, beeping, gently seeping,
Seeping through the conference door.
"'Tis only from the hall," I muttered. "A passerby it must implore."
"Only hall noise, nothing more."
Nonetheless the noise persisted. Its entreaties I resisted,
Till my boss at last insisted, "Find the source! My ears are sore!"
So through purses we did burrow. Pockets, wallets, all were furrowed,
Seeking just to find a cure. Oh! Cure, oh, for that noise before
We all went mad from more, more, more.

All at once my cheeks turned cherry, for the noise 'twas I did
carry,
Carry on my small Blackberry. I hit the switch, it beeped no
more …
So that now, to still the beating of my heart, I stood
repeating,
'Tis a message worth deleting, just an ad, or little more.
Some bulk e-mail, drug, or store—
This is it, and nothing more.
Presently my fear grew stronger; hesitating then no longer,
Glancing down, I had to, had to read what was the score.
I cast a look down as if nodding, to avoid my boss's
prodding
And the jeers of peers applauding, applauding me—the local
boor.
So I looked for words of text there, on the screen I can't
ignore—
Darkness there, and nothing more.
Deep into that darkness peering, long I stood there wondering,
fearing,
Doubting, dreaming dreams no mortal ever dared to dream
before;
Was the Blackberry just broken? Would the darkness give no
token?
Was this just some evil joke and should I throw it to the
floor?
This I wondered, should I throw it to the floor?!
Merely this, and nothing more.
Then I noticed each head turning, in the meeting, staring,
burning,
Soon again I turned so red, yes, redder than I was before.
"Surely," said I, "surely something live or dead, yes;
Let me see then, what the threat is, and this mystery
explore—
Let my heart be still a moment and this mystery explore;

Just blank screen, and nothing more!"
Open here I then rebooted, as the crowd sat quiet, muted,
And there flickered on the screen the messages of days of
    yore.
Not a single one I clicked on; not a clear response would flick
    on;
But, as if it had been kicked on, turned to gray. "My God," I
    swore;
And on cue my boss let loose and sent me packing out the
    door
Still no message; nothing more!
So I called the 1-800, and the phone rang then I blundered,
Pushing "one" instead of getting human help at "four."
Not the slightest slack was given; to the wrong place I was
    driven;
Like a demon unforgiven, sent me to the sales desk floor—
Where I got no help, no more—
On hold, and sat, and nothing more.
Then my cubemate came and queried, "What's with you? You
    don't look cheery?"
By the grave and stern decorum of the countenance I wore,
"I just fouled up in my big meeting." The whole story then
    repeating—
It all felt so self-defeating, hearing the whole thing once
    more—
"And I'm still on hold to fix it, fix it and find out the score
Of my message. *What's It For?!*"
Was it project change I dreaded? Was some work to Hades
    headed?
Was my subject matter expert vetted? Vetted as a fraud or
    more?
Was the customer agreeing that no living human being
Ever would be blessed with seeing finished product out the
    door?

Messages of doom or gloom or worse unseen and yet in store.
Could I read them? Nevermore.
But no message, and no ringing could be heard, no respite bringing
That one text, as if to share it would undo the pain that came before.
Nothing further of that message—no disaster did it presage.
Nothing; not a single vestige of the word I waited for.
"On the morrow it will function, function as it has before."
Said my cubemate, "Nevermore."
"Prophet!" said I, "thing of evil!"—prophet still, if man or devil!—
Whether tempter sent, or whether tempest tossed thee here ashore,
Desolate yet all undaunted, on this desert land enchanted—
This cell phone by horror haunted—tell me truly, I implore:
Is there—*is* there balm in Gilead?—tell me—tell me, I implore!
Quoth the cubemate, "Nevermore."
"Come on, man, you've bigger troubles than your cell phone (which is rubble).
You get back downstairs on the double—fixing up that 'meeting war.'
The boss is one unhappy master whom unmerciful disaster
Will invoke on you much faster, faster than he's done before—
'Cause you interrupted him with tech toys (better thing if you had snored
Or had thrown up on the floor)."
So I went back, looking mournful, wishing I had not been born, full
Knowing he would be so scornful, for the cell phone he abhorred.
"Sorry for the interruption, didn't plan on *that* disruption.

Or the message's corruption, stopping what you had in
  store."
One cold stare is all he shot me. Shot me—cutting to the
  core.
"Sit down," he said, and little more.
And then, as if on Satan's cue, the beeping started all anew
With fervency that cut right through the cold chill he was
  working for.
A hundred messages to tag you, flowing forth from this
  Niagara,
Selling cases of Viagra, timeshares, condos, Web sites,
  more.
"Wait! Wait!" I cried, "I'll shut it off, Never to be heard from
  more!"
And still security kept pushing, pushing me out the front
  door.
Quoth my *ex*-boss, "Nevermore."

* * *

Yes, Virginia, There Is a Project Manager

Ripped off from the Editorial Page, New York Sun, **1897**

(December 2004)

I am thirty-eight years old. Some of my co-workers tell me
there are no real project managers. But my boss tells me, "If
you see it on the Web site www.projectconnections.com, it's
so." Please tell me the truth, are there real project managers?
Virginia Noh

Virginia, your co-workers are wrong. They have been
affected by the skepticism of a skeptical age. They do not believe
except what they have seen happen in their organizations in
the past. They think that nothing can be which has not been

done in the organization for years and years past. All minds, Virginia, whether they be management's or team members', may be limited by their experience. In this great universe of ours, a single team member or stakeholder is a mere insect, an ant, in his intellect as compared with the boundless world about him, as measured by the intelligence capable of grasping the whole of truth and knowledge.

Yes, Virginia, there are real project managers.

They exist as certainly as plans and hope and strategies exist, and you know that they abound and give to your organization its greatest joys and achievements. Alas! How dreary would be the world if there were no project managers! It would be as dreary as if there were no Virginias. There would be no faith in deadlines, no objectives, no clear specifications and budgets to make possible the lofty dreams of humankind. We should have no vision, except in sense and sight. The structures, plans, and designs that take human vision from empty pits to inspiring skyscrapers would be extinguished.

Not believe in project managers! You might as well not believe in status reports. You might get your team to review every network diagram and Gantt to find evidence that the project managers aren't authentic, but even if you found an errant application of a tool, what would that prove? Few ever see the project managers doing their most important work, but that is no sign that there are no real project managers. The most real work in the world includes those things that neither management nor team members can see. Did you ever see a project manager coaching someone to help grow in the organization? Did you ever see a project team agonize over a team member's personal loss? Probably not, but that's no proof that they are not working. Nobody can conceive or imagine all the effort and strains there are unseen and unseeable in the world.

You tear apart the baby's rattle and see what makes the noise inside, but there is a veil covering our projects that hides the hours of coordination and planning and consternation that go behind every inch of forward progress. It is not by Monte Carlo or Microsoft Project that such efforts move forward. Faith in team members, nurturing of management, and appreciation for the customer all unite to push aside the curtain of misunderstanding and incomprehension to view the beauty and glory of a better future. Is it all real? Ah, Virginia, in all this world few things else are as real and abiding.

No project managers? Thank PMI they continue to find new ways to add value to our organizations and our day-to-day lives. A thousand years from now, Virginia, nay ten times 10,000 years from now, the fruits of their labors will continue to brighten the path to our futures.

Merry Christmas and a Happy New Year!

Note: The Francis P. Church editorial, "Yes Virginia, There Is a Santa Claus" (*New York Sun,* 1897) is one of the most famous editorials ever written. It was reprinted by the *Sun* for more than fifty years. Virginia O'Hanlon graduated (B.A., Hunter College) when she was twenty-one. She earned a master's from Columbia and later a doctorate from Fordham University. She taught and later served as a principal in the New York City school system until her retirement in 1959. Virginia regularly received mail about her Santa letter and replied with printed copies of the original editorial. She passed away at the age of eighty-one.

References/Bibliography

Ammer, Christine. *The American Heritage Dictionary of Idioms.* Boston, Massachusetts: Houghton Mifflin Harcourt, 2003

Association for Project Management. *APM Body of Knowledge, 5th Edition.* Bedfordshire, UK: Association for Project Management, 2006

Ayto, John. *Brewers Dictionary of Phrase and Fable, 17th Edition.* New York, New York: Collins, 2006

Barnhart, Robert. *Chambers Dictionary of Etymology.* London, UK: Chambers, 1999

Bossidy, Larry and Charan, Ram. *Execution: The Discipline of Getting Things Done.* New York, New York: Crown Business, 2002

British Standards Institution. *BS PD 6079-4: 2006 Project Management Guide to Project Management in the Construction Industry.* London, UK: British Standards Institution, 2006

Carr, M., S. Kondra, et al. 1993. Taxonomy-Based Risk Identification. *SEI Technical Report* CMU/SEI-93-TR-006.

Collins, Jim. *Good to Great: Why Some Companies Make the Leap...and Others Don't.* New York, New York: Collins Business, 2001

Defense Systems Management College. *A Competency Model of Program Managers in the DOD Acquisition Process.* Fort Belvoir, VA: Defense Systems Management College, 1990

Dhiegh, Khigh. *The Eleventh Wing.* Los Angeles, California: Dell Publishing, 1974

Dickens, Charles. *A Christmas Carol.* London, UK: Chapman and Hall, 1843

Fitzgerald, Edward. *The Rubaiyat of Omar Khayyam.* New York, New York: Penguin, 1995

Fleming, Quentin and Joel Koppelman. 2004. Sarbanes-Oxley and Earned Value Management. *Contract Management* 44:26–28

Haine, Edgar. *Railroad Wrecks.* Cranbury, New Jersey: Associated University Presses, 1993

Hedgpeth, Dana. 2008. Lockheed Faulted for Failure to Control Costs. *Washington Post* June 4, 2008: D-1

Hillson, David. 2002. "Use a Risk Breakdown Structure to Understand Your Risks." *Proceedings of the Project Management Institute Seminars and Symposium* Austin, Texas, 3–10 October, 2002. Project Management Institute. Newtown Square, Pennsylvania

International Organization for Standardization. *ISO 9000:2005 Quality Management Systems—Fundamentals and Vocabulary.* Geneva, Switzerland: International Organization for Standardization: 2005

International Organization for Standardization. *ISO 9001:2008 Quality Management Systems— Requirements.* Geneva, Switzerland: International Organization for Standardization: 2008

International Organization for Standardization. *ISO 9004:2000 Quality Management Systems—Guidelines for Performance Improvements.* Geneva, Switzerland: International Organization for Standardization: 2000

International Organization for Standardization. *ISO 10005:2005 Quality Management Systems—Guidelines for Quality Plans.* Geneva, Switzerland: International Organization for Standardization: 2005

International Organization for Standardization. *ISO 10006:2003 Quality Management Systems— Guidelines for Quality Management in Projects.* Geneva, Switzerland: International Organization for Standardization: 2003

International Organization for Standardization. *ISO 10007:2003 Quality Management Systems—Guidelines for Configuration Management.* Geneva, Switzerland: International Organization for Standardization: 2003

Maney, Kevin. *The Maverick and his Machine: Thomas Watson, Sr. and the Making of IBM.* Hoboken, New Jersey: John Wiley and Sons, 2003

Previts, Gary John. 1996. The First Century of the CPA. *Journal of Accountancy* October 1, 1996

Project Management Institute. *A Guide to the Project Management Body of Knowledge, Third Edition.*

Newtown Square, Pennsylvania: Project Management
Institute, 2004

Project Management Institute. *A Guide to the Project
Management Body of Knowledge, Fourth Edition.*
Newtown Square, Pennsylvania: Project Management
Institute, 2008

Random House. *Random House Dictionary of the English
Language, Unabridged.* New York, New York: Random
House, 1987

Standards Australia. *The Australian/New Zealand
Standard for Risk Management (AS/NZS 4360).*
Sydney, Australia: Standards Australia, 2004

Thayer, Ernest. *Casey at the Bat.* Chicago, Illinois:
McClurg and Company, 1912

Tuckman, B. 1965. Developmental Sequence in Small
Groups. *Psychological Bulletin 63: 384–399*

Vaughan, Diane. *The Challenger Launch Decision: Risky
Technology, Culture and Deviance at NASA.* Chicago,
Illinois: University of Chicago Press, 1997

Vroom, Victor. *Work and Motivation.* Hoboken, New
Jersey: Wiley, 1964

Wilhelm, Richard and Baynes, Cary, trans. *The I Ching
or Book of Changes.* Princeton, New Jersey: Princeton
University Press, 1967

Zemke, Ron and Schaaf, Dick. *The Service Edge.* New
York, New York: Plume, 1990

INDEX

226